# Internet for Windows:
## America Online Edition

## Other Prima Computer Books

Cruising America Online
1-2-3 for Windows: The Visual Learning Guide
Excel 4 for Windows: The Visual Learning Guide
Excel 5 for Windows: The Visual Learning Guide
PowerPoint: The Visual Learning Guide
Windows 3.1: The Visual Learning Guide
Word for Windows 2: The Visual Learning Guide
Word for Windows 6: The Visual Learning Guide
WordPerfect 6 for Windows: The Visual Learning Guide
WinFax PRO: The Visual Learning Guide

## Upcoming Books!

Procomm Plus for Windows: The Visual Learning Guide
ACT! 2.0 for Windows: The Visual Learning Guide
Word 6 for the Mac: The Visual Learning Guide
Excel 5 for the Mac: The Visual Learning Guide

## How to Order:

Individual orders and quantity discounts are available from the publisher, Prima Publishing, P.O. Box 1260BK, Rocklin, CA 95677-1260; (916) 786-0426. For quantity orders, include information on your letterhead concerning the intended use of the books and the number of books you wish to purchase.

# Internet for Windows:
## America Online Edition

**Grace Joely Beatty, Ph.D.**

**David C. Gardner, Ph.D.**

**David A. Sauer, M.S.**

Prima Publishing
P.O. Box 1260BK
Rocklin, CA 95677-1260

Managing Editor: Paula Munier Lee
Acquisitions Editor: Sherri Morningstar
Project Editor: Andrew Mitchell
Cover Production Coordinator: Anne Flemke
Copyeditor: Becky Whitney
Production: Blue Moon Design
Indexer: Katherine Stimson
Book Designer: Blue Moon Design
Cover Designer: Page Design, Inc.

America Online is a registered service mark of America Online, Inc.

If you have problems installing or running America Online, notify America Online, Inc. at phone number: (800) 827-3338. Prima Publishing cannot provide software support.

ISBN: 1-55958-554-4
Library of Congress Card Number: 94-065730
Printed in the United States of America
95 96 97 98 RRD 10 9 8 7 6 5 4 3 2 1

# Acknowledgments

We are deeply indebted to reviewers around the country who gave generously of their time to test every step in the manuscript. Shirley Beatty, David Coburn, Steve Godfrey, Tom and Maura Healey, Carolyn and Ray Holder, Peter Meltzer, and Steve Meltzer cannot be thanked enough!

Linda Beatty and Joshua Gardner worked with us and did more than their fair share of beta testing, editing, relinking, and renaming. In addition, Linda Beatty created the original artwork. Thanks, Linda, for going above and beyond the call of duty with the spell-check chapter.

Special thanks to Pam McGraw, of AOL, for her support and the accounts for our beta testers. Pam put us in touch with George Thomson and Luis Montiel, our technical advisors, who were more than generous with their time and expertise. Additional thanks go to Steve Godfrey, of Next Generation Software, for his spell-check program.

We are personally and professionally delighted to work with everyone at Prima Publishing, especially Sherri Morningstar, editor; Andrew Mitchell, project manager; Mike VanMantgam, publicity coordinator; and Anne Johnson, cover production.

Linda Miles and Nora Cate McArdle, our technical editors, came through under incredible time pressures! Thanks, Linda Miles, for sticking with us through ten Visual Learning Guides! Blue Moon Design added wonderful features to the design of the book and did the layout and color separations. Paul Page created a wonderful cover design.

Bill Gladstone and Matt Wagner, of Waterside Productions, created the idea for this series. Their faith in us has never wavered.

Joseph and Shirley Beatty made this series possible. We can never repay them. Asher Schapiro has always been there when we needed him.

Paula Gardner Capaldo and David Capaldo have been terrific. Thanks, Joshua and Jessica, for being great kids! Our project humorist, Mike Bumgardner, is a riot!

We could not have met the deadlines without the technical support of Ray Holder, our electrical genius, and Diana Balelo, Frank Straw, Daniel Terhark, and Martin O'Keefe, of Computer Service & Maintenance, our computer wizards.

# Contents

# Customize
# Your Learning

*Prima Visual Learning Guides* are not like any other computer books you have ever seen. They are based on our years in the classroom, our corporate consulting, and our research at Boston University on the best ways to teach technical information to nontechnical learners. Most important, this series is based on the feedback of a panel of reviewers from across the country who range in computer knowledge from "panicked at the thought" to sophisticated.

Each chapter is illustrated with color screens to guide you through every task. The combination of screens, step-by-step instructions, and pointers makes it impossible for you to get lost or confused as you follow along on your own computer.

We had several challenges in writing *Internet for Windows: America Online Edition*. The first was that not only is AOL's program constantly changing. The second was that Internet itself is reborn from moment to moment. The folks at AOL work hard at creating new features and upgrading existing ones, and they are very good at their jobs. This is wonderful for users, but it does mean that the screens you see in this book may not look *exactly* like what you see because of the frequent upgrades to the program and the ever-changing nature of the Internet. However, the directions will still work. To protect the innocent, we changed the Internet addresses that appear in the chapters.

We truly hope that you'll enjoy using the book, the America Online program, and joining the millions of folks who have reached out to each other around the globe. Let us know how you feel about our book, and whether there are any changes or improvements we can make. You can contact us through Prima Publishing at the address on the title page or send us an e-mail letter. Our Internet address is Write.Bks@aol.com. Thanks for buying the book. Enjoy!

David, Joely, and David

## PART I: SETTING UP AOL FOR THE INTERNET

### CHAPTER

# Installing America Online

Before you can begin your Internet adventure, you must have America Online installed and set up to get you on the information superhighway. This chapter and the one that follows are designed to do just that. In this chapter, you will do the following:

❖ Install America Online
❖ Move the program icon to another group
❖ Delete the America Online group window

## GETTING STARTED

1. **Make** a **backup copy** of your American Online diskette.

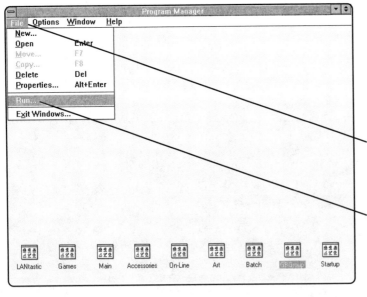

2. **Insert** the America Online **diskette** in **drive a** (or b).

3. **Type win** at the C prompt (c:<) to open Windows if it is not already open.

4. **Click** on **File** in the menu bar. A pull-down menu will appear.

5. **Click** on **Run**. The Run dialog box will appear.

## INSTALLING THE PROGRAM

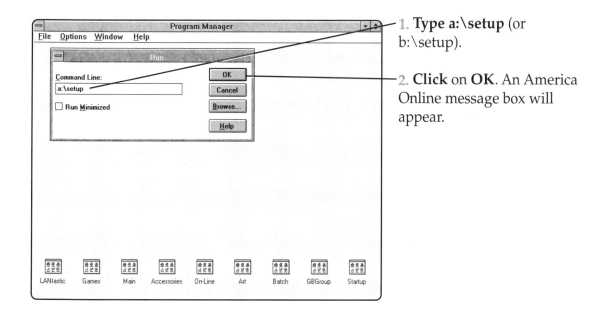

1. **Type a:\setup** (or b:\setup).

2. **Click** on **OK**. An America Online message box will appear.

This message box will hang around while America Online's setup program checks out your computer.

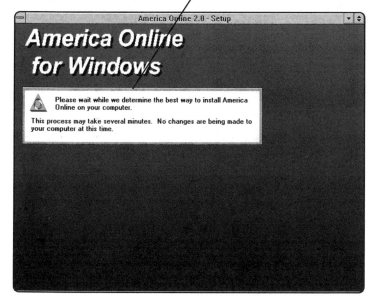

Next, An America Online Setup dialog box will appear.

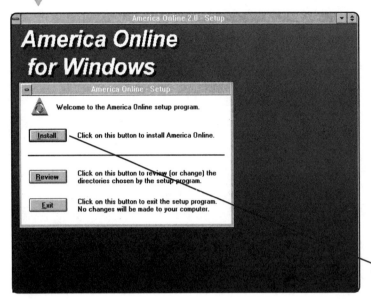

If you have a previous version of America Online installed and do *not* want to transfer your address book and preferences to the new version, click on Review. Another dialog box will appear with options. Follow the directions on the screen. After following the directions, the dialog box shown below will appear.

3. If you are new to AOL (or you *do* want to transfer your address book and preferences to this new version) **click** on **Install**. Another America Online dialog box will appear.

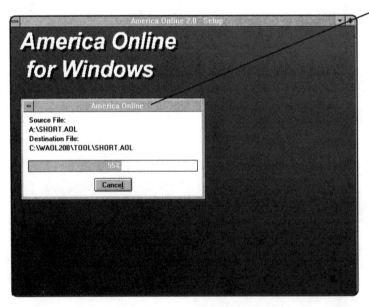

This dialog box will keep you informed of the progress of the installation. Once all the files are copied, the America Online Install dialog box will appear.

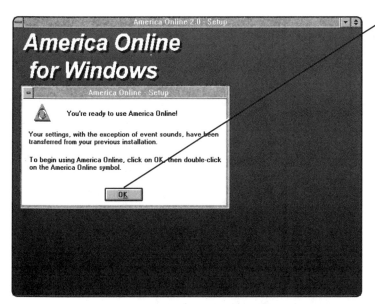

4. **Click** on **OK**. The dialog box will close. Voilá! The installation is complete.

## MOVING AOL'S PROGRAM ICON TO ANOTHER GROUP

The steps in this section and the next one are optional but highly recommended. We like to put our most-used program icons into one group to minimize the number of group icons.

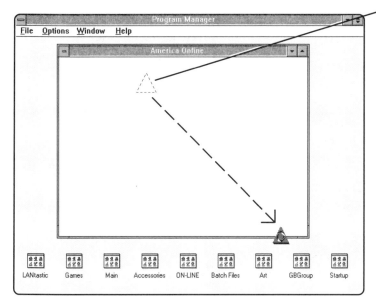

1. **Place** the **mouse arrow** on **top** of the AOL icon.

2. **Press** and **hold** the **mouse button** and **drag** the **icon** toward the group in which you want to place the AOL icon. In this example, we're putting the AOL icon in GBGroup.

3. **Release** the **mouse button** when the icon is on top of the group icon. The America Online icon will disappear into the group icon and will be housed in that group.

## DELETING THE AMERICA ONLINE GROUP WINDOW

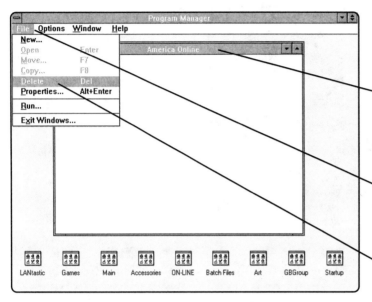

The America Online window is now empty, so you can delete it.

1. **Click** on the America Online **title bar** to make sure that it is the active window.

2. **Click** on **File** in the menu bar. A pull-down menu will appear.

3. **Click** on **Delete**. The Delete dialog box will appear.

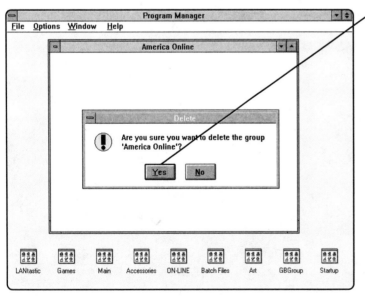

4. **Click** on **Yes**. The America Online (AOL) group window will disappear forever. Your AOL program icon is now located in the group in which you placed it.

You are now ready to go to Chapter 2 to set up America Online so that you can easily access the information superhighway.

# Setting Up America Online

America Online (AOL) has made it easy for you to set up your computer to automatically dial an AOL local number and immediately connect to the Internet through the America Online Internet Center. In this chapter, you will do the following:

❖ Find a list of local access numbers near where you live
❖ Select a local access number and an alternate number
❖ Dial your local access number and connect to America Online
❖ Choose a screen name and enter a password
❖ Enter America Online as a fully installed member
❖ Create a second screen name

## FINDING AN ACCESS NUMBER

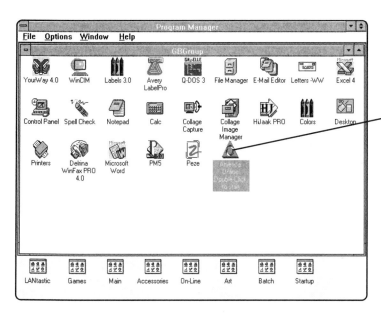

1. **Open** the **group window** where the AOL program icon is located, if it is not already open.

2. **Click twice** on the **AOL program icon**. After a long intermission, a Welcome to America Online dialog box will appear.

**3.** **Click** on **Yes** *if you match the standard setup* described on the screen. Another welcome to America Online dialog box will appear. It is shown on the top of the next page. The screen below will not appear.

**OR**

**Click** on **No** *if you don't match the standard setup* described here. The Set up America Online dialog box will appear.

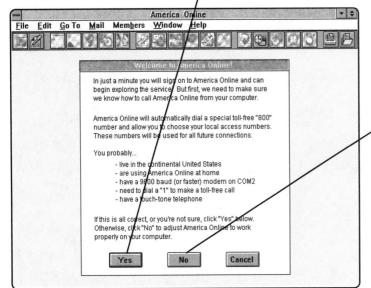

## Customizing Dialing Options

**1.** **Type** the appropriate **number** (e.g. 9,) if you need to dial a number to get an outside line.

**2.** **Click** on **OK**. The Welcome to America Online dialog box will appear. It is shown on the top of the next page.

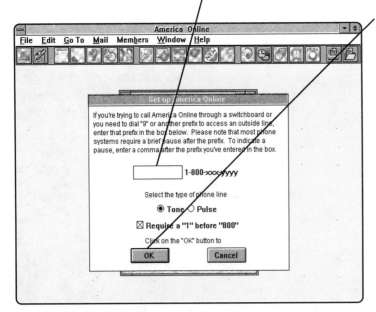

## Dialing the 800 Number

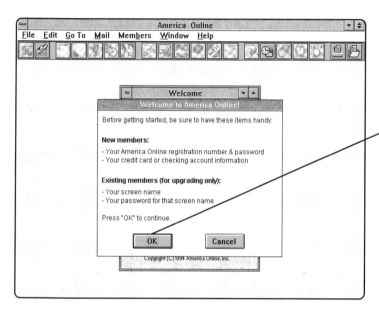

In this section, America Online will dial an 800 number automatically to provide you with a list of local telephone numbers.

1. **Click** on **OK**. An America Online dialing status dialog box will appear.

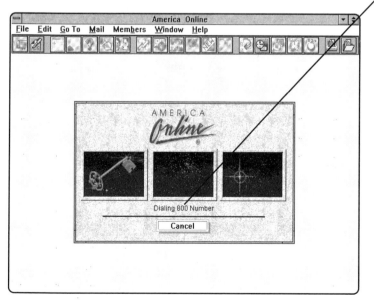

This line in the status box will show the progress of the dialing and connecting operation. Once the connection is made (it may take a while), a Welcome to America Online dialog box will appear.

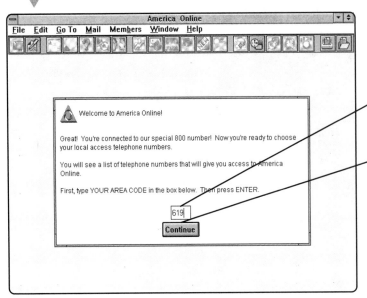

## Selecting a Local Number — First Choice

1. **Type** your **area code** in the box.

2. **Click** on **Continue**. The Choose Local Access Number - First Choice dialog box will appear.

3. **Click** on the appropriate **telephone number** to highlight it. You can change this number if you find a less expensive number later on. See Chapter 3, "Supercharging America Online," for directions on changing this access number or the baud rate at which you connect.

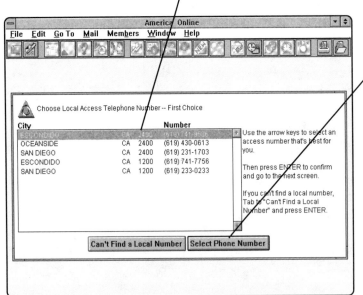

4. **Click** on **Select Phone Number**. The screen shown at the botttom of the next page will appear.

**OR**

**Click** on **Can't Find a Local Number**. The screen shown at the top of the next page will appear.

# Trying Again

**1.** If you clicked on Can't Find a Local Number in the previous screen, **repeat steps 1 through 4** on the previous page. We couldn't find a local number that didn't require a toll charge. In the end, we made a deal with the phone company to give us a reduced rate for our access number. America Online is growing rapidly, and at some point there should a local access number for everyone.

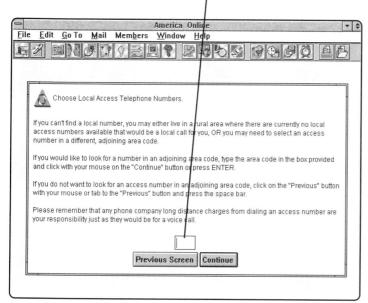

# Selecting a Local Number — Second Choice

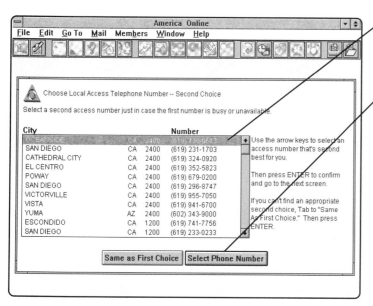

**1. Click** on the **alternate telephone number**, if there is one, to highlight it.

**2. Click** on **Select Phone Number** or **Same As First Choice**. The Confirm Your Access Number Choices dialog box will appear.

Make certain that these are the telephone numbers you want to use.

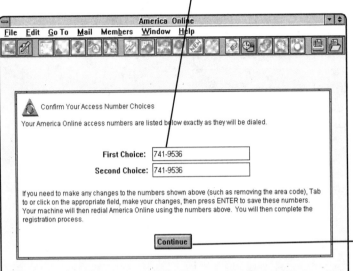

**3. Type** the **correct phone number(s)** in the appropriate boxes if these are not correct.

# DIALING THE LOCAL ACCESS NUMBER

**1. Click** on **Continue**. The America Online status dialog box will appear.

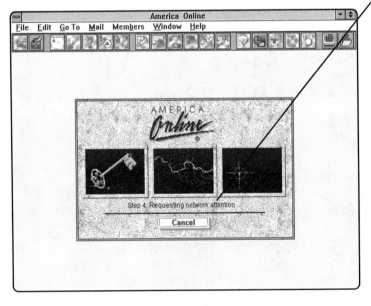

This line will give you a continuous update of the dialing and connecting process. Once the dialing and connecting is complete, the Welcome to America Online dialog box will appear.

## Thinking Ahead

In the next two sections, you will need:

❖ Your certificate number

❖ A credit card for billing

## ENTERING THE CERTIFICATE NUMBER AND PASSWORD

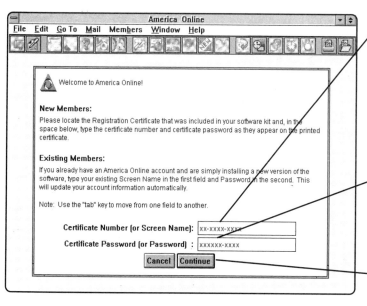

1. **Type** the **certificate number** that came with your software in the Certificate Number box and **press Tab**. The cursor will move to the Certificate Password box.

2. **Type** the **password** that came with your software in the Certificate Password box.

3. **Click** on **Continue**. The Getting Around dialog box will appear.

## ENTERING PERSONAL DATA

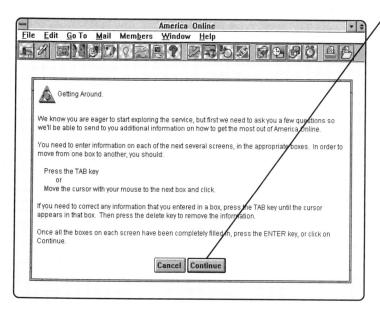

1. **Click** on **Continue**. An information fill-in dialog box will appear.

**2. Type** your **first name** and **press** the **Tab key**. The cursor will move to the Last Name text box.

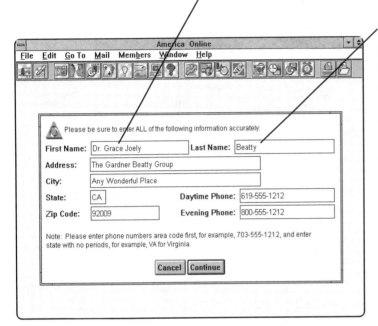

**3. Type** your **last name** and **press** the **Tab key**. The cursor will move to the Address text box.

**4. Repeat steps 2 and 3** until you have entered all the information.

## CHOOSING A BILLING METHOD

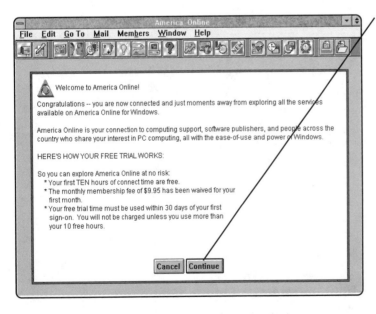

**1. Click** on **Continue**. Another Welcome to America Online dialog box will appear. It will not be shown here. After reading the information about AOL's fees on that screen, **click** on **Continue** again. The Billing Options dialog box will appear.

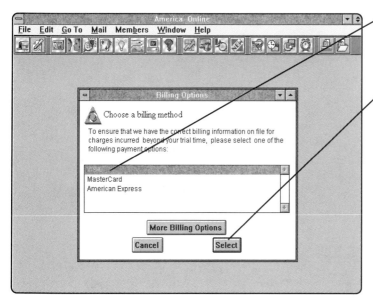

2. **Click** on the **billing method** of your choice to highlight it.

3. **Click** on **Select**. A credit-card information screen will appear. (It will not be shown here.) After you have typed your billing information on that screen, **click** on **Continue**. The Choosing a screen name dialog box will appear.

## CHOOSING A SCREEN NAME

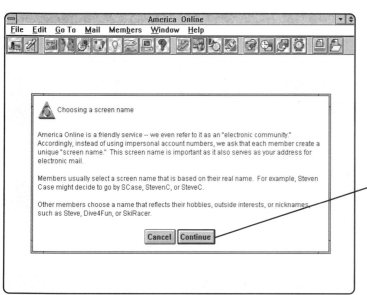

Your screen name is like a CB radio handle—much more fun than a bunch of numbers separated by periods or commas! You may not be able to get your first choice, so have several ideas.

1. **Click** on **Continue**. Another Choosing a screen name dialog box will appear.

A screen name must have:

❖ A letter, not a number, as the first character

❖ A minimum of three characters and no more than ten.

❖ Any combination of letters, numbers and spaces (e.g., S Case22).

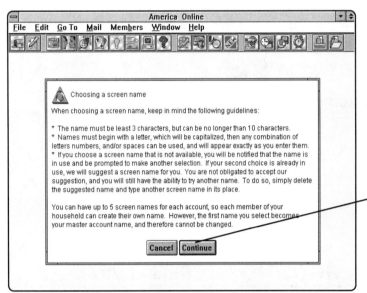

2. **Click** on **Continue**. Another Choosing a screen name dialog box will appear.

3. **Type** a **screen name**.

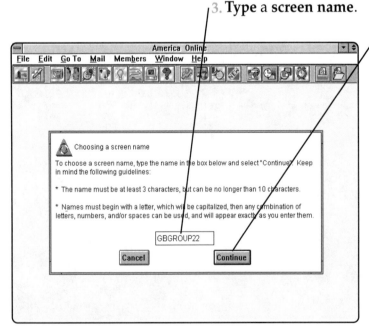

4. **Click** on **Continue**. The Choosing a password dialog box will appear.

**Note**: You may have to repeat this process several times if someone else has already chosen "your" screen name.

## CHOOSING A PASSWORD

A password should be:

❖ Easy to remember! (It's a good idea to write it down and hide it someplace, just in case)

❖ *Not obvious* to anyone

❖ At least four but no more than eight characters.

❖ Any combinations of letters and numbers

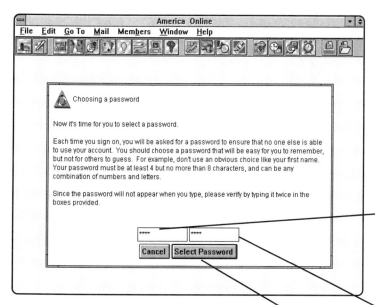

1. **Type** your **password** and **press** the **Tab key**. The cursor will move to the next password box.

2. **Type** the *same* **password** again.

3. **Click** on **Select Password**. A How to Explore America Online dialog box will appear.

## ENTERING AMERICA ONLINE

1. **Click** on **Continue**. Another How to Explore America Online dialog box will appear.

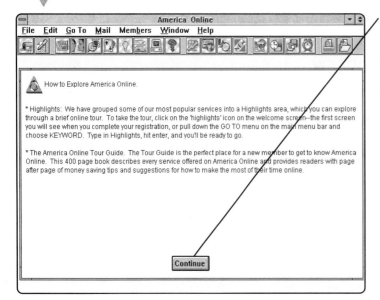

**2. Click** on **Continue**. Would you believe that another Welcome to America Online dialog box will appear?

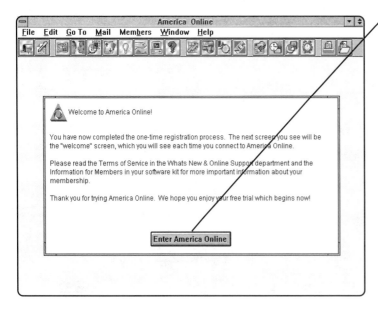

**3. Click** on **Enter America Online**. The Welcome to America Online window will appear. Notice that, while AOL boots up, you will see the Main Menu before you see the Welcome screen. At last! We thought we would never get there.

America Online is positively a great program and a fun place to be. However, some of these opening dialog boxes can get pretty boring.

# CREATING A SECOND SCREEN NAME

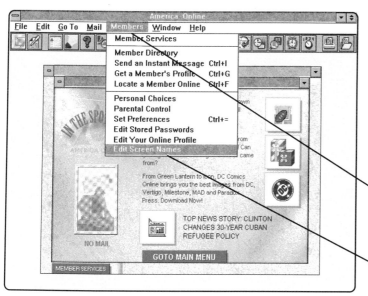

As an AOL member, you can have up to five different screen names under one account. You can create individual screen names for your children or create a special screen name for a mailing list.

**1. Click** on **Members** in the menu bar. A pull down menu will appear.

**2. Click** on **Edit Screen Names**.

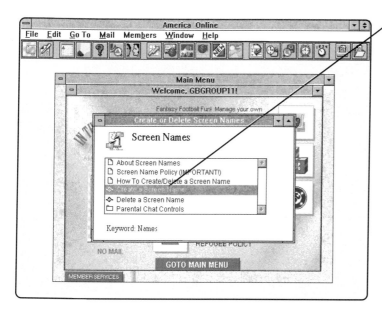

**3. Click twice** on **Create A Screen Name**. A Create a Screen Name dialog box will appear.

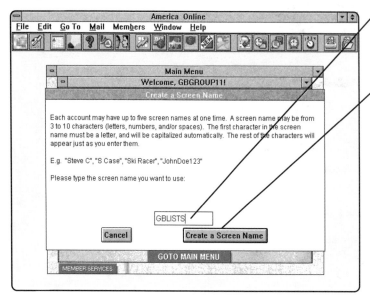

**4.** Type a **screen name**. In this example, we use the name "GBLISTS."

**5.** Click on **Create a Screen Name**. A Set Password dialog box will appear.

**Note:** If a dialog box appears with the message, "The name you requested is already in use. Please try another name," **click** on **OK** and choose a different screen name.

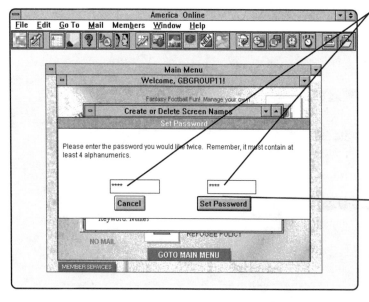

**6.** Type the **password** you want to use in the first text box, then repeat the *same password* in the second text box. You can use the same password that you used for your first screen name, or you can use a different password.

**7.** Click on **Set Password**. An America Online dialog box will appear.

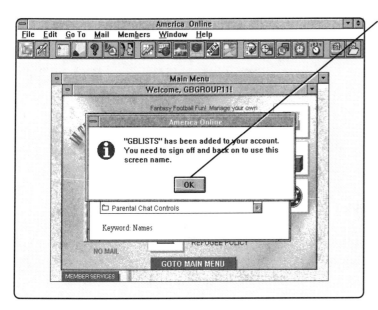

**8. Click** on **OK**. Your new screen name has now been added to the AOL database.

**Note:** In order to activate this screen name, you will first have to sign off. After you have signed off, the Goodbye From America Online dialog box will appear.

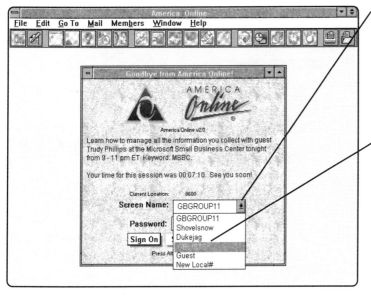

**9. Click** on the ⬇ next to your original screen name. A pull down menu containing a list of screen names and sign on options will appear.

**10. Click** on the **new screen name**. It will replace the screen name currently located in the screen name text box. You are now ready to sign on with your new screen name!

# Supercharging America Online

Okay, cyberspace cadets, here's your chance to supercharge America Online. We'll show you how to automate your password so that you don't have to enter it every time you sign on. We'll also show you how to switch to a faster baud rate.

*Baud rate* is a measure of the speed at which data is sent over telephone lines. America Online is set up initially to work at a 2400 baud rate. If you bought your modem in the last year, it can probably accommodate 9600 or even 14,400 baud rates. That's the good news. The bad news is that you cannot always access a high-baud telephone number during peak hours. Therefore, it's a good idea to keep the 2400 baud setting as a backup for those times when the telephone lines are jammed. In this chapter, you will do the following:

❖ Automate your password
❖ Find a local telephone number that has been set up to handle a 9600 baud rate
❖ Create a second setting for the 9600 line

## AUTOMATING YOUR PASSWORD

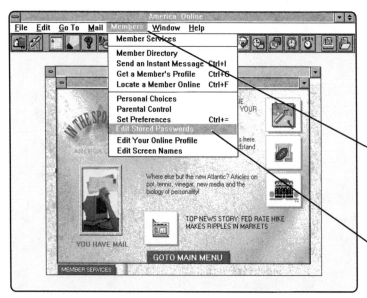

You can set up America Online so that you don't have to enter your password each time you sign on. You must be signed on to start the process.

1. After you're signed on, **click** on **Members** in the menu bar. A pull-down menu will appear.

2. **Click** on **Edit Stored Passwords**. A dialog box will appear.

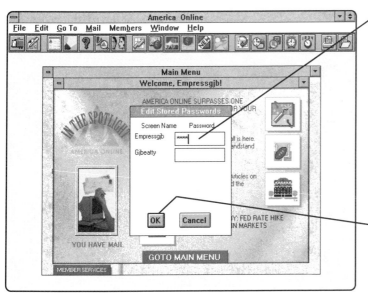

**3. Type** your **password** in the box next to your screen name.

If you have more than one screen name for this account, you can automate each one, or you can automate only the main account, as you see in this example.

**4. Click** on **OK**.

## GOING TO THE 9600 BAUD ACCESS CENTER

AOL has set up telephone numbers in your area that will work at different baud rates. In this section, you will look for numbers that work at a 9600 baud rate. At present, there are no AOL numbers set up to work at a 14,400 baud rate. This may have changed by the time you read this book.

**1. Sign on to AOL**, if you haven't already done so.

**2. Click** on the **Keyword icon** in the toolbar. It's the seventh icon from the right. The Keyword dialog box will appear.

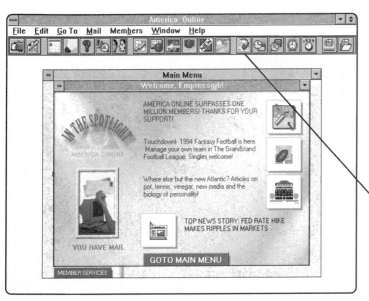

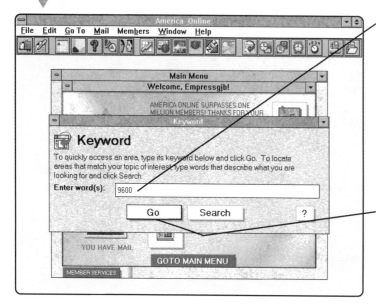

**3. Type 9600** in the Keyword box. (You can try typing 14,400 to see if AOL has incorporated the faster rate into its setup. If you get a message that says the keyword is not valid, simply highlight 14,400 and type 9600 to replace it.)

**4. Click** on **Go**. You'll see the America Online message box below.

**5. Click** on **Yes** to go to the 9600 Baud Access Center.

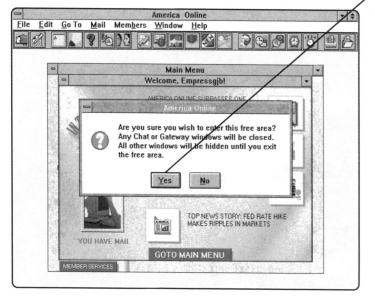

## SEARCHING FOR AN ACCESS NUMBER IN YOUR AREA CODE

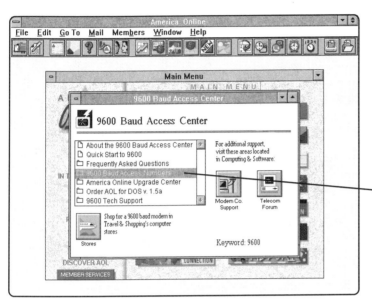

AOL has set up numbers with various carriers, such as AT&T, Sprint, and Tymnet, to accommodate different baud rates. In this section, you'll search for an appropriate access number in your area code.

1. **Click twice** on **9600 Baud Access Numbers**. Another dialog box will appear.

2. **Click twice** on **Search Access Numbers**. The Search Access Numbers dialog box will appear.

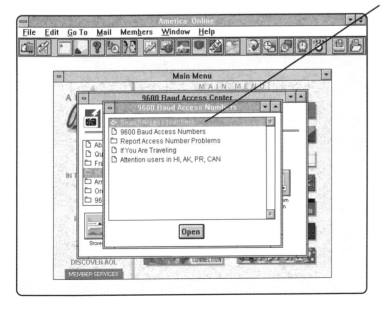

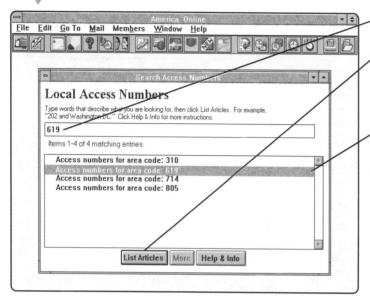

3. **Type** your **area code**.

4. **Click** on **List Articles**. You'll see a list like the one shown here.

5. **Click twice** on **your area code** in the list. A list of all access numbers for your area code will appear, as you'll see in the next example.

Amazingly, you can't highlight the correct number in this next screen and then click on some button and have AOL transfer the number to the appropriate spot. You actually have to resort to pen and paper for this next step!

6. **Write down** the **location**, **telephone number**, and **carrier** of the city or town closest to you. Notice that there may be several numbers that can handle 9600 bauds.

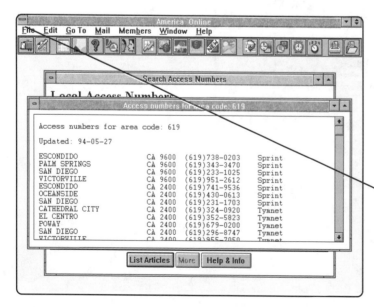

## SIGNING OFF

The next section requires that you be signed off from AOL. However, you don't have to close the program itself—simply "disconnect."

1. **Click twice** on the **Control menu box** (▭) on the left of the America Online title bar. You'll see an America Online message box.

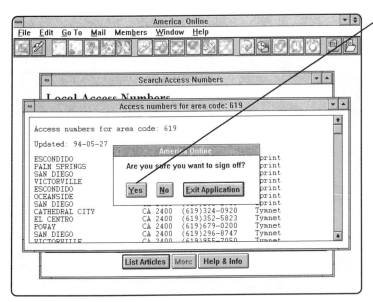

2. **Click** on **Yes**. You will be disconnected from AOL, but the program itself will remain on your screen.

## SETTING UP A FASTER ACCESS NUMBER

AOL allows you to establish different settings, or *locations*, with different baud rates and different telephone numbers. For example, you can use different telephone numbers for your personal account vs. your business account.

Notice that AOL is set up to show a current location of "Home" for the 2400 baud rate. In this section, you'll create a second "location" for the 9600 baud access number.

Notice also that the Password box is no longer on your screen because you don't need to type your password anymore.

1. **Click** on **Setup**. The Network and Modem Setup dialog box will appear.

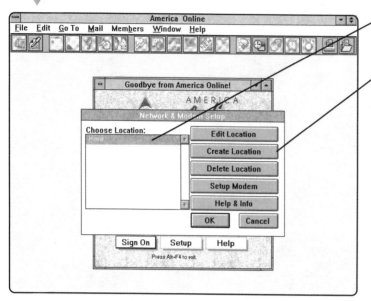

Notice the Home location for the 2400 baud rate.

**2.** **Click** on **Create Location**. The Network Setup dialog box will appear.

**3.** **Type 9600** in the Location box. (You can also type "office" or someone's name. The purpose is to identify the second setting you are creating.)

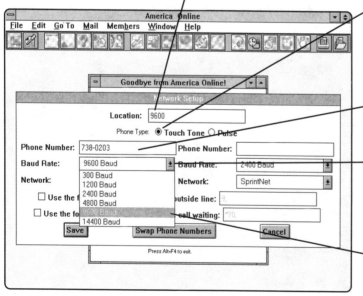

**4.** **Click** on the **appropriate phone type** to put a dot in the circle. In this example, it is Touch Tone.

**5.** **Type** the **phone number** you wrote down.

**6.** **Click** on the ⬇ to the right of the Baud Rate box. A pull-down list of baud rates will appear.

**7.** **Click** on **9600 Baud**. The list will disappear and 9600 Baud will be in the text box.

8. **Click** on the ⬇ to the right of the Network box and select the appropriate telephone carrier.

## Setting Dialing Options

Connecting to any online service can be frustratingly slow during peak hours. AOL automatically dials twice. You can set it to dial the same number twice or set up a different number for the second dial. We've found that dialing the same number twice often gets us connected.

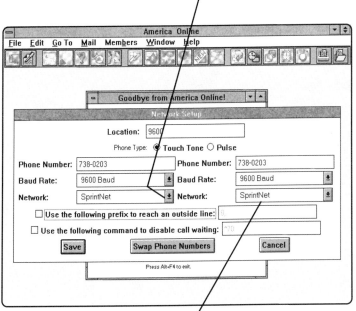

1. **Repeat steps 5 through 8 above** to enter the correct information in the second set of boxes. In this example, the information is the same because we want AOL to dial the same number twice.

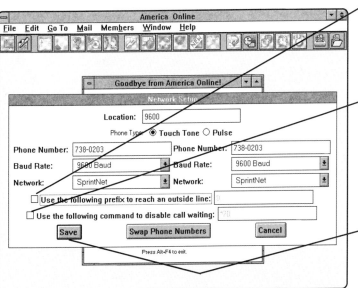

2. If you have to dial a prefix to reach an outside line, **click here**. The number 9 will appear.

3. If you are using a single line for your telephone and your modem and you have call waiting, **click here** to disable call waiting during modem operation.

4. **Click** on **Save**. The Network & Modem Setup dialog box will reappear.

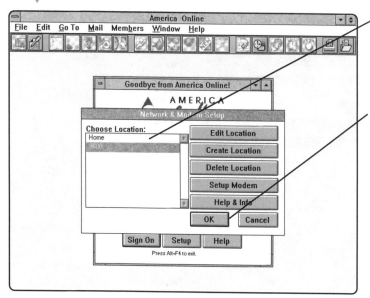

Notice that both the Home (2400 baud) and 9600 baud locations are in the Network & Modem Setup dialog box.

**5. Click** on **OK**. The dialog box will close.

Notice that the Current Location is now 9600.

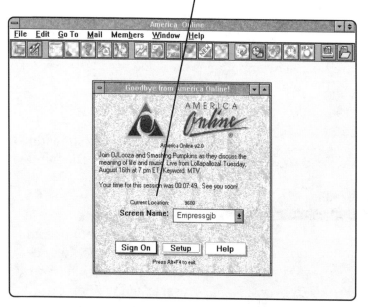

During peak hours, you may not be able to sign on to AOL at 9600 baud. If you switch back to 2400 baud, it can be easier to sign on. You may wonder, "Why not just stay at 2400 baud?" The answer is that 9600 baud enables AOL to work faster. Moving around in AOL is faster, getting and sending mail is faster, and uploading and downloading files is faster.

However, if you find that you cannot connect to AOL at 9600 baud, see the next page to switch back temporarily to the 2400 baud setting.

## Switching Back to 2400 Baud

Sometimes you can't log on to AOL at the 9600 baud rate no matter how many times the modem dials. It's easy enough to switch back to 2400 baud.

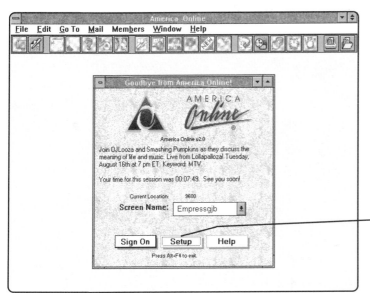

If you're following along in this chapter, you may not want to actually switch back to 2400 baud at this time. Keep this section for future reference.

1. Before you sign on to AOL, **click** on **Setup**. The Network & Modem setup dialog box will appear.

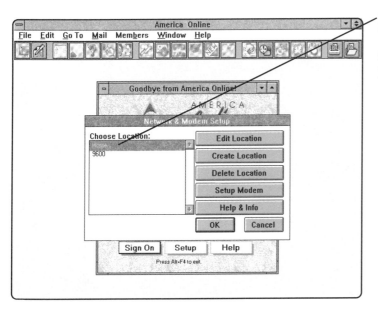

2. **Click twice** on **Home**. You'll come back to this screen with the Home, or 2400, baud location.

## SIGNING ON TO AOL WITH AN AUTOMATED PASSWORD

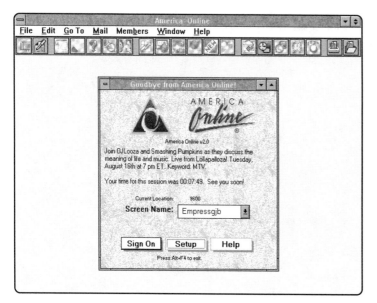

Now that you've automated your password, you can sign on to AOL even more easily than before.

**1. Press Enter** or **click** on **Sign On**. America Online will begin the sign-on process.

# Customizing AOL for the Internet

The Internet is not an integral part of America Online, and America Online has no control over the Internet's content. However, America Online gives you economical access to the Internet. AOL also helps you use the Internet's vast sea of information in a way that few services can. In this chapter, you will do the following:

❖ Gain an understanding of how you are connected to America Online
❖ Gain an understanding of how AOL connects with the Internet
❖ Learn how AOL helps you use the Internet's resources
❖ Customize the Go To menu for rapid access to the Internet services

## UNDERSTANDING HOW YOU ARE CONNECTED TO AOL

America Online is a huge computer that is connected to your computer and more than 1,000,000 other personal computers by telephone lines and modems. As an AOL member, you can use all AOL services. These services include the ability to talk to other members through AOL's computer as well as send mail to other America Online members.

The example on the next page describes how one of the services, electronic mail (e-mail), works in America Online.

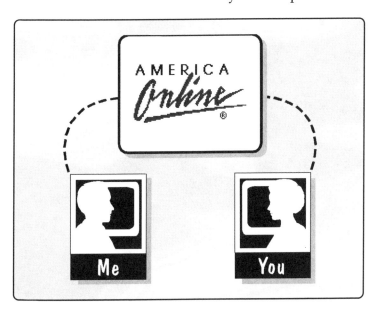

## Sending E-Mail Through AOL

When you join America Online, it's like moving into a new town. This "town," called AOL, includes people from all over the country.

❶ When you send e-mail to your friend Jessica, who is also an AOL member, it goes to the AOL computer. The AOL computer is like your local post office.

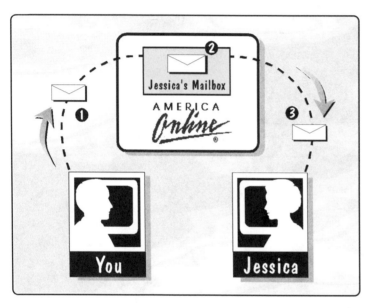

❷ AOL puts the letter in Jessica's box at the post office.

❸ Jessica can read your letter on her screen when she reads her mail. She can print the letter, save a copy of the letter to her hard drive, forward a copy of your letter to someone else, and reply to your letter.

All these functions are done through America Online's computer. The mail doesn't leave America Online. In terms of our post office example, your letter was handled by your local post office and did not leave your town.

You use the Internet when you want to send a letter to someone who's not on AOL or, to continue our example, when you want to send mail to someone who doesn't live in your town. A simplified view of the Internet is on the next page.

# THE INTERNET: A SIMPLIFIED VIEW

The Internet was originally developed by the government as a communications network for government agencies, universities, and research centers. Individuals don't normally have direct access to the Internet because the cable connection is expensive. However, individuals can become members of online services, such as AOL, that have a connection to the Internet.

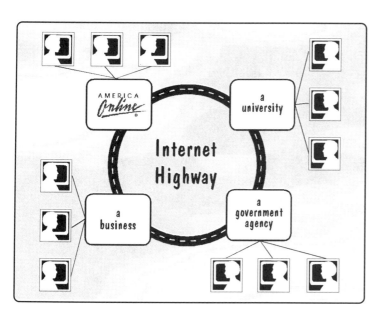

Once you have access to the Internet, you can communicate with some 20 million computers around the world. Amazing, isn't it?

The diagram shown here is a simplified overview of Internet connections:

❖ AOL and other online services, universities, and government agencies are just a few examples of organizations connected to the Internet.

❖ These organizations (and their members) can communicate with each other by way of the Internet highway that connects them. This means that you, as a member of AOL, can connect into a university library in Germany, a commercial database, or a special NASA-funded computer, for example.

Let's take a look at what happens when you send e-mail through the Internet.

## Sending E-Mail on the Internet

When you send electronic mail to someone who's not on AOL, it's like sending a letter across the country (or to another country). Your letter goes first to your local post office. Your local post office then sends the letter to your friend's post office. The Internet is the highway that connects the post offices.

In this example, you send mail to Josh, who is not a member of AOL but who is at Boston University and has a student Internet address through the university. This is what happens:

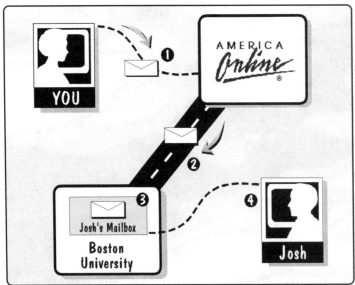

❶ The mail goes first to the AOL computer, your home-town post office.

❷ America Online knows by the address that Josh doesn't live in your home-town, so it sends the mail by superhighway (the Internet) to Boston University's computer post office.

❸ Boston University's post office puts the mail in Josh's mailbox.

❹ When Josh logs on to his Internet account at B.U., he has a message saying that he has mail. He can read it, print it, save it, and forward it just as Jessica did when she received your letter through AOL.

The next two pages will provide a very quick overview of five ways in which you can use the Internet through America Online.

# INTRODUCING AOL'S
# INTERNET CONNECTION

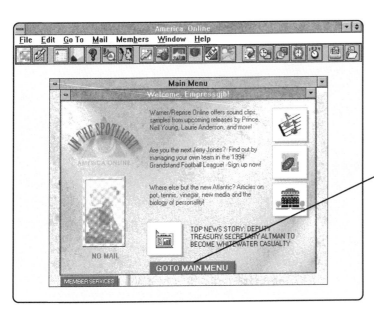

You must be signed on to America Online to use the Internet Connection. There are several ways to get to the Internet Connection. One way is to use the Main Menu.

**1. Click** on **GO TO MAIN MENU**. The Welcome screen will be sent to the background, and the Main Menu will be brought to the foreground.

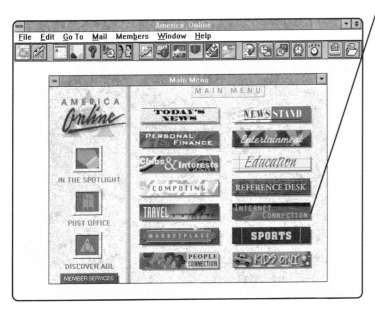

**2. Click** on **Internet Connection**. You'll see an hourglass as AOL makes the connection. The Internet Connection dialog box will appear on your screen.

## VIEWING INTERNET FEATURES

There are five ways to use the Internet on AOL. In this section we'll simply *introduce* you to each of the five functions. Each function is discussed in step-by-step detail in the remaining sections of this book.

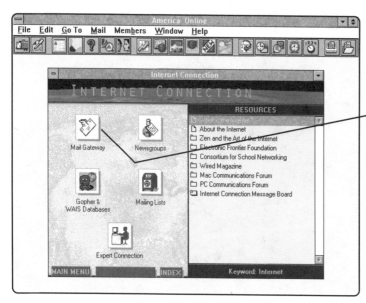

### Using the Mail Gateway to Send and Receive Mail

**1. Click** on the **Mail Gateway icon.** The Mail Gateway dialog box will appear.

See Chapters 5 through 8 for details on sending and receiving Internet mail. Chapter 9 contains directions on getting and using a shareware spell-check program for online mail. If you're like us and send business correspondence through the Internet, you may well be interested in making sure that your letters don't contain spelling errors.

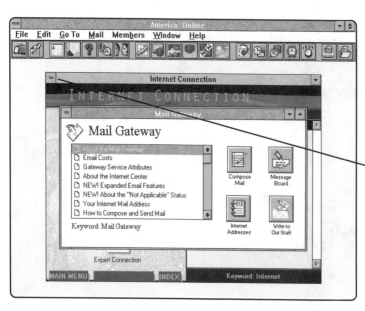

**2. Click twice** on the **Control menu box** (⊟) to close the Mail Gateway dialog box and return to the Internet Connection.

# Subscribing to an Internet Newsgroup

A newsgroup has nothing to do with the news. It is an electronic discussion group where members can post mail messages on specific topics and respond to messages posted from other members. Each newsgroup is based on a specific topic, and there are literally thousands of topics from which to choose.

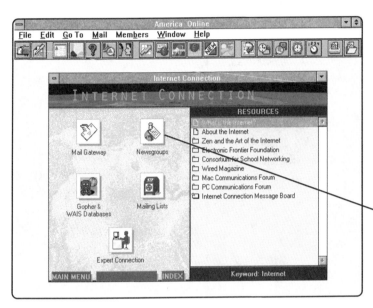

1. **Click** on the **Newsgroups** icon. The Newsgroups dialog box will appear.

See Chapters 12 and 13 for details on signing on to, contributing to, and resigning from an Internet newsgroup.

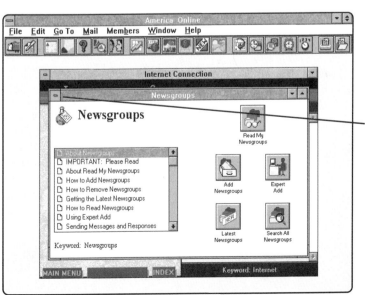

2. **Click twice** on the **Control menu box** (□) to close the Newsgroups dialog box and return to the Internet Connection.

# Searching for Information Using Internet Gopher

Gopher and WAIS let you hook into the databases on other computers and search for information. You cannot, of course, hook into personal computers, like yours and mine, that don't have a direct connection to the Internet. You can, however, hook into special computers that do have a direct connection to the Internet and have been set up as searchable databases. You can hook into computers at resource sites such as the Library of Congress or the NASA Goddard Space Flight Center, or go to computers that have business information, games, or genealogy information, for example.

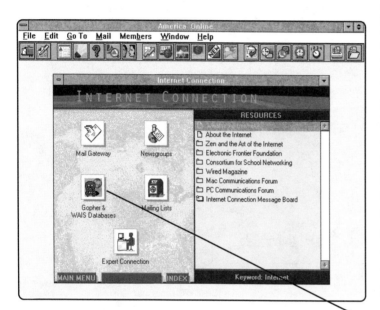

**1. Click** on the **Gopher & WAIS Databases** icon. The Gopher & WAIS dialog box will appear.

See Chapters 14 through 17 for details on researching business topics, term-paper topics, and even finding a job.

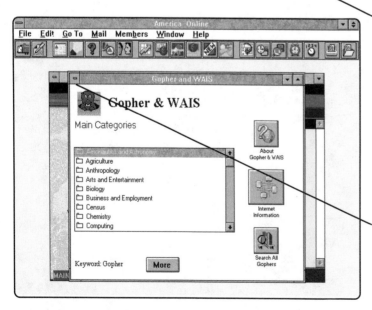

**2. Click twice** on the **Control menu box** (☐) to close the Gopher & WAIS dialog box and return to the Internet Connection.

# Subscribing to an Internet Mailing List

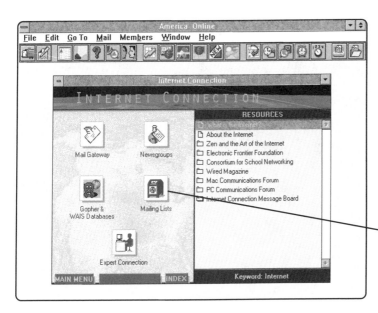

A mailing list is another type of electronic discussion group, much like newsgroups. Like newsgroups, there are thousands of mailing lists, or topics, from which to choose. The major difference between mailings lists and newsgroups is the way you get messages.

1. **Click** on the **Mailing Lists icon**. The Internet Mailing Lists dialog box will appear.

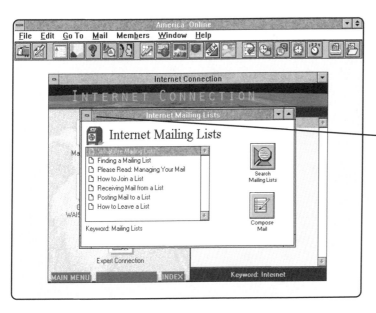

See Chapters 10 and 11 for details on signing on to, contributing to, and resigning from an Internet mailing list.

2. **Click twice** on the **Control menu box** (□) to close the Internet Mailing Lists dialog box and return to the Internet Connection.

## Using Expert Connection to Send and Receive Documents on the Internet

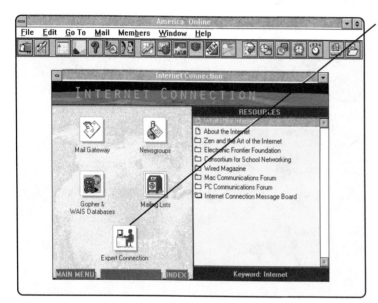

Currently, you cannot send documents and graphic files on the Internet through America Online. The AOL staff is busy working on the Expert Connection interface.

See Chapter 18 for an introduction to what this feature will be like when it is installed.

## SPEEDING UP THE CONNECTION WITH VARIOUS INTERNET FEATURES

You can use the Internet Connection to click your way into the various Internet features. This process requires multiple clicks, as you experienced in the above example. If you're a real speed demon, you can customize America Online to allow you even faster access to Internet features. In the following pages, you'll customize the Go To menu.

## CUSTOMIZING THE GO TO MENU FOR THE INTERNET

Now you're ready to customize America Online so that you can get to the Internet functions quickly from anyplace in America Online. In this section, you'll customize the Go To menu so that you can access the AOL Internet Connection's options more quickly than the previous procedure allowed.

**1. Click** on **Go To** in the menu bar. A pull-down menu will appear.

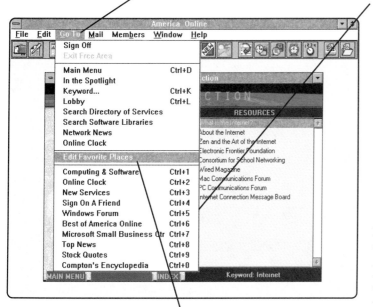

In this example, notice that there are ten items at the bottom of the pull-down menu. These have been set up by AOL to boot you directly into each of these features. You can customize these items to reflect the choices you want. In this section, you'll customize the first two items to be Internet features. On our menus, we've customized a total of three items on the pull-down menu. You can change the items on the pull-down menu at any time, so if you don't like the way we've customized the menu, you can change it to suit the way you work.

**2. Click** on **Edit Favorite Places**. The Favorite Places dialog box will appear.

3. When the Favorite Places dialog box opens, the cursor appears at the end of Computing & Software in the first box. **Press and hold** the **mouse button** and **drag** the cursor to the **left** to highlight Computing & Software.

4. **Type Internet Gopher** and **press** the **Tab key**. The cursor will move to the Keyword text box. Internet Gopher will now be the first item on the list. Don't be concerned about losing the ability to search for computing information and software on AOL. You can get to each of these features in numerous ways, and, besides, we'll move "Computing & Software" to another position on the list a little later.

Using a Keyword is another way to access an Internet function. You'll learn to use a Keyword in Chapter 5. Right now, you'll enter the appropriate keywords into the list so that you can use the keyword function if you choose.

5. Because the cursor is already flashing at the end of Computing, **click twice** to highlight the word. **Type Gopher**. "Gopher" is the keyword for Gopher & WAIS Databases.

**6. Repeat steps 3 to 5** to insert the following entries into the left and right columns of the Go To Menu:

Line 2: Internet Newsgroups　　Newsgroups

When you're through, the first two items in the Favorite Places section of the Go To menu will be Internet functions. You can access them from wherever you happen to be in AOL without having to go to the Internet Connection.

**7.** Unless you plan on signing up lots of friends, **change Sign On A Friend** in line 4 **to Computing & Software**. Remember, you can always use the keyword Friend to access this function. Erasing an item from this list doesn't affect your ability to access the feature in numerous other ways.

Line 4,
**Computing & Software**
Line 6, Keyword
**Computing**

**8. Click** on **Save Changes**. The dialog box will close and you'll be back at the Internet Connection screen.

---

**America Online**

File　Edit　Go To　Mail　Members　Window　Help

Favorite Places

| Key | Menu Entry | Keyword |
|-----|-----------|---------|
| 1 | Internet Gopher | Gopher |
| 2 | Internet Newsgroups | Newsgroups |
| 3 | New Services | New |
| 4 | Sign On A Friend | Friend |
| 5 | Windows Forum | Windows |
| 6 | Best of America Online | Best of AOL |
| 7 | Microsoft Small Business Ctr | MSBC |
| 8 | Top News | Top News |
| 9 | Stock Quotes | Stocks |
| 10 | Compton's Encyclopedia | Encyclopedia |

Save Changes　　　　　Cancel

---

**America Online**

File　Edit　Go To　Mail　Members　Window　Help

Favorite Places

| Key | Menu Entry | Keyword |
|-----|-----------|---------|
| 1 | Internet Gopher | Gopher |
| 2 | Internet Newsgroups | Newsgroups |
| 3 | New Services | New |
| 4 | Computing & Software | Computing |
| 5 | Windows Forum | Windows |
| 6 | Best of America Online | Best of AOL |
| 7 | Microsoft Small Business Ctr | MSBC |
| 8 | Top News | Top News |
| 9 | Stock Quotes | Stocks |
| 10 | Compton's Encyclopedia | Encyclopedia |

Save Changes　　　　　Cancel

## Using the Customized Menu

Now you're ready to see how easy it is to access the Internet with your newly customized menu.

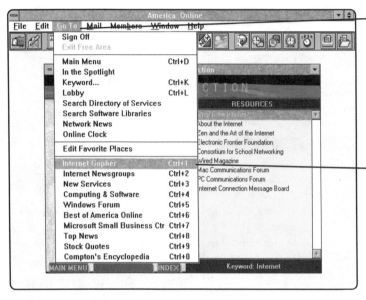

**1. Click** on **Go To** in the menu bar. A pull-down menu will appear.

Notice that there are now two Internet options in the menu.

You can click on either of these features to go immediately there. It may seem silly to be doing this when the Internet Connection dialog box is on your screen, but remember, the purpose of customizing the Go To menu was to make it easy to access these functions from wherever you are in America Online.

## SWITCHING TO THE MAIN MENU

You can switch back to the Main Menu from anyplace in AOL.

**1. Click** on **Window** in the menu bar. A pull-down menu will appear, showing a list of all open windows.

**2. Click** on **Main Menu**.

# SIGNING OFF FROM AOL WITHOUT CLOSING THE PROGRAM

You can exit America Online from anywhere in the program. In this example, however, you'll sign off without exiting from AOL. This will take you off-line but leave AOL on your screen. This will also allow you to go directly to Chapter 5 and compose mail off-line.

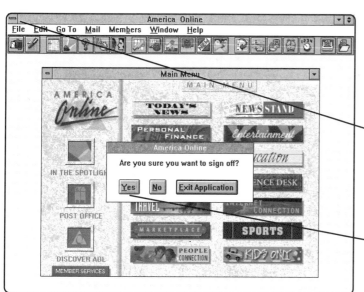

1. **Click twice** on the **Control menu box** (⊟) on the left of the AOL title bar. An America Online dialog box will appear.

2. **Click** on **Yes** to shut down your modem connection but leave the AOL program running. AOL will be open on your screen, but you won't be signed on.

If you click on Exit Application, you'll exit from AOL completely.

If you click on No, you'll cancel the Exit command.

**CHAPTER**

**5**

# Sending Internet E-Mail

You can use America Online's mail service to send electronic mail to anyone in the world whose computer is on the Internet or who has an account on another online service, such as CompuServe or AppleLink. You don't have to go to the Internet Connection to send Internet mail. You can send Internet mail with the standard America Online Compose Mail dialog box. Because charges can add up quickly, we recommend that you compose your mail messages off-line before you sign on to America Online. In this chapter, you will do the following:

❖ Save money by composing mail off-line
❖ Send to one or more people
❖ Send carbon copies
❖ Read mail sent
❖ Print a copy of mail sent
❖ Save mail to a special directory
❖ Get the Internet mail address of your representative in Congress

## OPENING AMERICA ONLINE

In this example, the icon for America Online was moved to a customized group window.

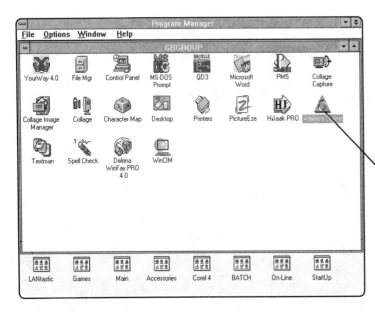

1. **Click twice** on the **America Online icon** to open the program.

## COMPOSING MAIL OFF-LINE

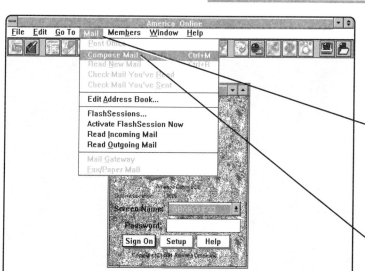

You can save money by composing your mail off-line before you sign on to America  Online.

1. Before you sign on to America Online, **click** on **Mail** in the menu bar. A pull-down menu will appear.

2. **Click** on **Compose Mail**. The Compose Mail dialog box will appear.

## DEALING WITH INTERNET ADDRESSES

The first rule of sending e-mail is to have the person give you his address. There is no easy way to look up someone's Internet address because there is no comprehensive directory of Internet names and addresses.

### Deciphering Internet Addresses

Internet addresses can be confusing at first glance, but they do follow a specific format. Let's take a closer look at the parts of the Internet address.

❶ The first part of the address is the person's name e.g. bbunny or efudd.

❷ The person's name is always followed by @, for "at."

The part of the address after the @ depends on how complicated the address is. For example, if you live in an apartment building, your address has more parts to it than if you live in a single house. You have to give your apartment number as well as your street address. The same is true of an Internet address. It helps to look at the last element in the address first.

## Examples of Internet Addresses

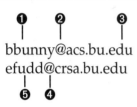

bbunny@acs.bu.edu
efudd@crsa.bu.edu

❸ The last element in these addresses is edu. This is one of six major categories that describe the types of Internet accounts. The six categories, or *domains*, are listed to the left. The "edu" domain name tells you that these are educational accounts.

## Internet Categories

COM = Commercial
EDU = Educational
GOV = Government
MIL = Military
NET = Networks
ORG = Organizations

You may also see 2-letter country codes, such as US for the United States, CN for Canada, JP for Japan

❹ The next part of the address (bu) tells you that this is a Boston University account.

❺ The two Boston University addresses have different letters after @ because Boston University has many different computers hooked to the Internet.

Each of these parts of the address is followed by a period (.), called a "dot" in online talk, or *dotspeak*. The dot separates the parts of the address. If you want to sound like one of the "in" crowd, read the first name above as "bbunny at acs dot bu dot edu."

## Making an Online Address into an Internet Address

As a member of AOL, you have to add elements to your AOL address to make it an Internet address. This is true of the addresses in all online services. For most online services, there is one simple formula:

---

**Making an Online Service Address Into an Internet Addresses**

❶ ❷ ❸ ❹❺

1234567@mcimail.com (an MCI Mail address)

WRITEBKS@AOL.COM (an AOL address)

Jeannie2@genie.com (a GEnie address)

21147.123@compuserve.com (a CompuServe address)

---

❶ Type the person's screen name or identification number (also called a user ID).

❷ Type @ after the individual's name.

❸ Type the name of the online service.

❹ Type a dot.

❺ Type com to identify it as a commercial service.

There are some things you should notice about these Internet addresses:

❖ It doesn't matter whether you type the name in all uppercase letters, all lowercase letters, or a combination. Addresses are not case sensitive. WRITEBKS is the same as WriteBks and writebks.

❖ A CompuServe user ID has a comma ( 21147,123). The Internet doesn't recognize commas, so the comma must be changed to a dot (i.e. 21147.123).

## ADDRESSING MAIL

You can send the same letter to more than one person.

1. **Type** the **Internet address** of the first person who will get the mail message. In this example, it is 76004.72@compuserve.com. Notice that a long name will automatically wrap to the next line.

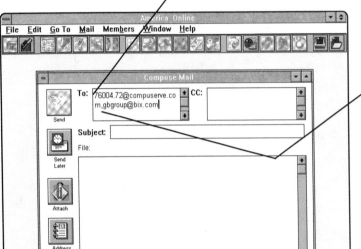

2. **Type** a **comma** to separate this address from the next.

3. **Type** the **Internet address** of the second person who will get this letter. In this example, it is gbgroup@bix.com. Don't put a space between the comma and the second name.

4. **Repeat steps 2 and 3** as many times as necessary. If you regularly send Internet mail to the same group of people, you can create a group name and include all appropriate people in the group. See the section entitled "Adding a Group Address" in Chapter 6.

**Note:** When you send AOL mail to multiple AOL recipients, AOL will list the names of all recipients on every person's copy of the letter. Internet mail does *not* do this. With Internet mail, the first person's message will show *only* that it is addressed to him. The second person's message will show *only* that it is addressed to her, etc. If you want people to know who else is getting the letter, type the list of names into your Internet message. See the next page for a discussion of original vs. carbon-copy recipients.

## Sending a Carbon Copy

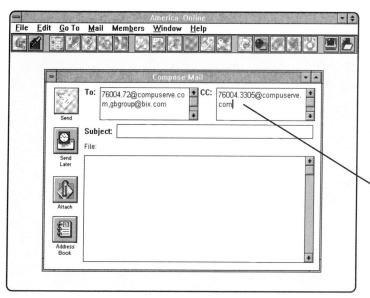

Even though AOL has a Carbon Copy (CC) box, it doesn't work with Internet mail at the present time. As with multiple recipients, a carbon-copy recipient will see his name as the only name in the To line.

1. **Type** a **carbon copy name** as you see here so that the person gets a copy of the letter. Also type a CC line at the end of your message with the names of people who received copies. This way, everyone will know who got copies.

Depending on your age, you may be asking, "What the heck is a carbon copy? If you want the person to get a copy, why not put the name in the To list?" The term *carbon copy* comes from the time when letters were typed on a typewriter and copies were made using a piece of carbon paper. Hence, a *carbon copy*. In terms of business etiquette, there is a difference between putting someone's name as a carbon-copy recipient vs. putting multiple names in the To line. Let's say that you are heading an interdepartmental project team and you want to send the final report to all involved department heads as well as to a department head who is not directly involved in the project. In terms of business etiquette, the names of involved department heads should be in the To line (perhaps in alphabetical order if they are all equal in rank), and the name of the other department head should be in the CC line.

## Typing a Subject and Message

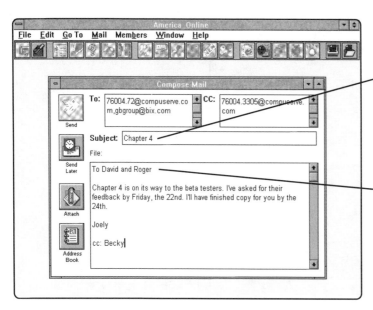

The Subject is a required field in Internet mail.

1. **Type** the **subject** of your message. It should have no more than 32 characters, although it can have spaces as part of the 32 characters.

2. **Press** the **Tab key** to move to the File field. **Type** your **message**. If your message is longer than 32K, which is about eight pages of text, you'll have to divide it and use several e-mails. Notice that this letter is addressed to two people and that a CC line is at the bottom. This way, everyone knows who got copies.

## Minimizing Your Message

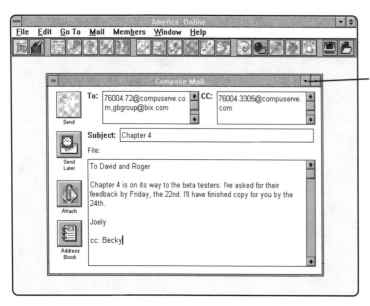

You have to be signed on to AOL to send mail.

1. **Click** on the **Minimize button** (▼) to minimize the Compose Mail dialog box to an icon at the bottom of your screen. The Welcome dialog box will reappear. You can write as many messages as you want before you actually sign on to AOL. As you finish each message, minimize it, click on Mail, click on Compose mail, and then start your next one.

## SIGNING ON TO AMERICA ONLINE

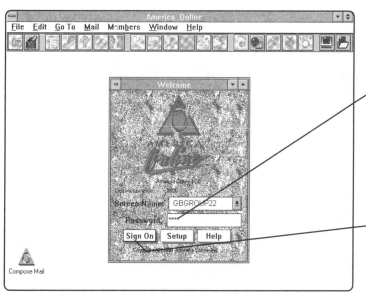

Now that you've finished composing mail, you're ready to sign on.

**1. Type** your **password**. If you automated your password (see the section "Automating Your Password" in Chapter 3), you don't have to do this step.

**2. Click** on **Sign On**. The America Online logo will appear as you hear the usual connecting noises.

## SENDING MAIL

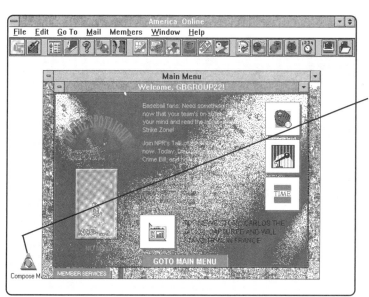

You must first maximize the Compose Mail icon so that you can send the mail.

**1. Click twice** on the **Compose Mail icon** at the bottom of your screen. The Compose Mail dialog box will appear on your screen with your mail message.

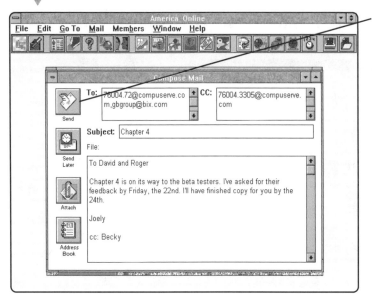

**2. Click** on **Send**. When your mail has been sent, you will see the message below.

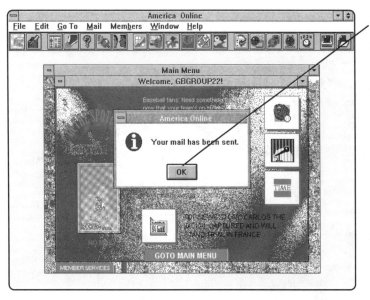

**3. Click** on **OK** to close this message box.

# READING OUTGOING MAIL

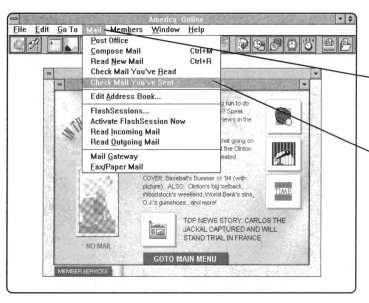

You can read mail you've sent.

**1. Click** on **Mail** in the menu bar. A pull-down menu will appear.

**2. Click** on **Check Mail You've Sent**. The Outgoing Mail dialog box will appear with a listing of mail you've sent.

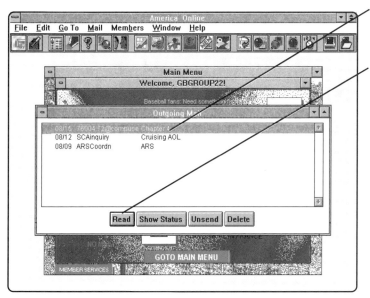

**3. Click** on the **mail** you want to read.

**4. Click** on the **Read button**.

**Note:** The Show Status and the Unsend buttons apply only to mail sent through AOL, so they won't do anything to Internet mail.

Mail will stay on this list for seven days. If you send lots of mail, you may want to use the Delete key to delete it sooner. The Delete key will simply delete the highlighted item from this list. It has no effect on the actual status of the mail that has been sent.

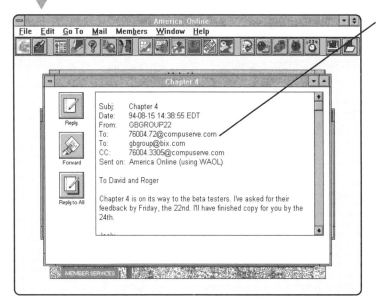

Notice that the multiple recipients and the carbon-copy recipient are shown in your AOL version of the letter, even though they will not be shown in the Internet version.

## PRINTING A LETTER

You can print a copy of outgoing mail after you have opened it in Read view, as you did in the section above.

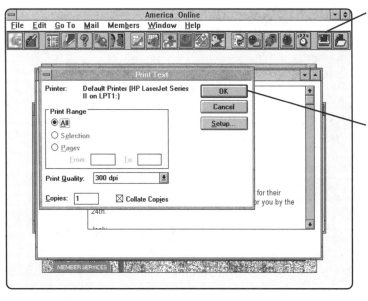

1. **Click** on the **Print icon**. It's the second one from the right. The print dialog box will appear, as you see in this example.

2. **Click** on **OK**. The letter will print.

## SAVING E-MAIL YOU'VE SENT

If you're sending business messages through e-mail, you'll want to save an electronic copy. Even if you're just having fun, it helps to have a record of what you said. We suggest that you create a special directory for your e-mail.

### Switching to File Manager

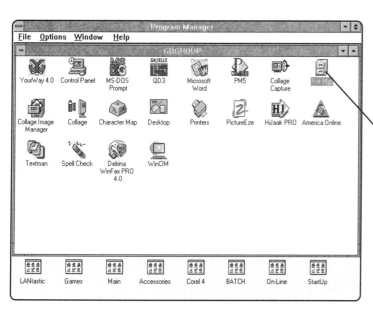

1. **Press and hold** the **Ctrl key** and **press** the **Esc key**. The Task List dialog box will appear, as you see in this example.

2. **Click twice** on **Program Manager**. The Program Manager will come to the foreground.

3. If necessary, **click twice** on the group icon on *your* system that contains your File Manager icon.

4. **Click twice** on the **File Manager icon**. The File Manager window will appear.

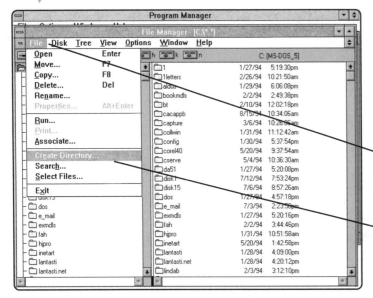

# Creating an E-Mail Directory

1. **Press** the **Home key** to go to the C:\ at the top of the Directories list.

2. **Click** on **File** in the menu bar. A pull-down menu will appear.

3. **Click** on **Create Directory**. The Create Directory dialog box will appear.

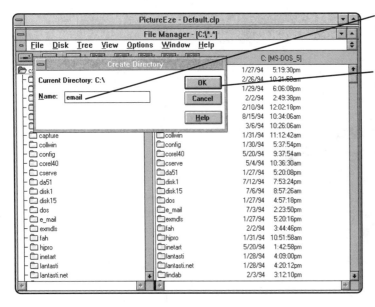

4. **Type email** in the Name box.

5. **Click** on **OK**. The dialog box will close and a directory entitled "email" will appear in the Directories list.

If you correspond with several people on a regular basis, create a subdirectory for each one. This makes it much easier to sort your mail and find it after you've filed it.

## Creating E-Mail Subdirectories

1. **Type** the letter **e**. The highlight bar will move to the first directory beginning with an *e*. If necessary, press the ↓ key to move the highlight bar to the newly created email directory.

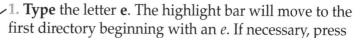

2. **Repeat steps 2 through 5** in the section "Creating an E-Mail Directory." Because the email directory is highlighted when you do this, you'll create a sub-directory with this process.

These are some examples of the subdirectories we have created for our e-mail.

Repeat the steps in the section "Switching to File Manager," earlier in this chapter, to go back to America Online.

You may have to reopen your letter in Read view.

## Saving a Letter

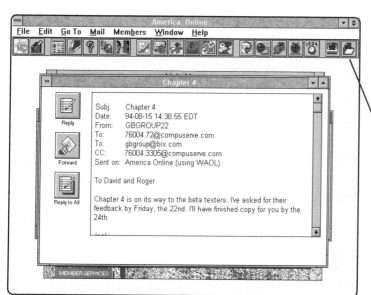

1. **Click** on the **Save icon**. It's the last one on the right. The Save Text As dialog box will appear.

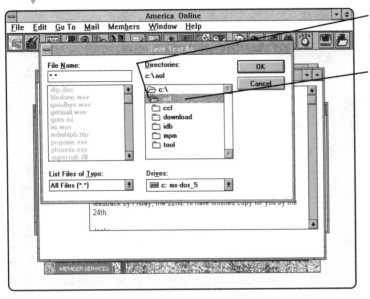

"aol" is the directory created by America Online.

**2. Click twice** on the **c:\** to show the entire directory list.

**3. Type** the letter **e** to go to the first directory beginning with *e*. If necessary, **press** the ⬇ to go to the email directory.

**4. Click twice** on **email**.

**5. Click twice** on the appropriate subdirectory of e-mail. The directory you selected will move up beneath email and show an open file folder. The other subdirectories will no longer be shown on the list.

**6. Type** a **filename plus** the **extension** of your word-processing program. Because we use Word, we save this file under a name such as roger522.doc.

**7. Click** on **OK**.

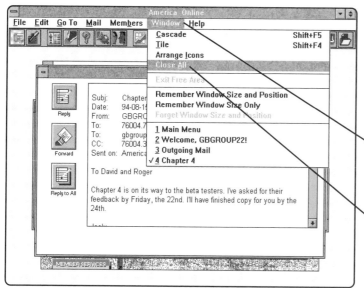

# CLOSING ALL WINDOWS

You can close all open windows very quickly.

**1.** **Click** on **Window** in the menu bar. A pull-down menu will appear.

**2.** **Click** on **Close All**. All windows will close and the Welcome window will be minimized to an icon at the bottom of your screen.

# CHANGING THE SAVE TO DIRECTORY

As you saw above, America Online is set up to save mail to the AOL directory. It will continue to go to the AOL directory even if you created an e-mail directory unless you change the working directory designation in the Preferences dialog box. Fortunately, this is easy to do. First, you have to minimize AOL so that you can get to Program Manager and the group that contains the AOL icon.

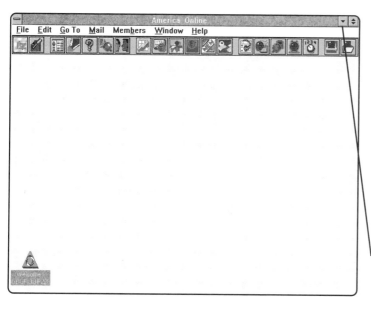

**1.** **Click** on the **Minimize button** (▼) on the right of the AOL title bar.

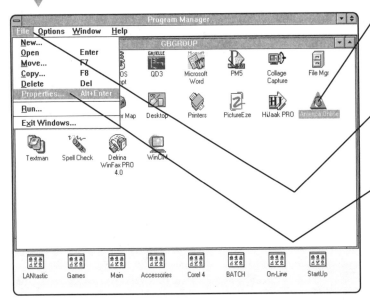

**2. Click** on the **America Online icon** in the group window. The name below the icon will be highlighted.

**3. Click** on **File** in the menu bar. A pull-down menu will appear.

**4. Click** on **Properties**. The Program Item Properties dialog box will appear.

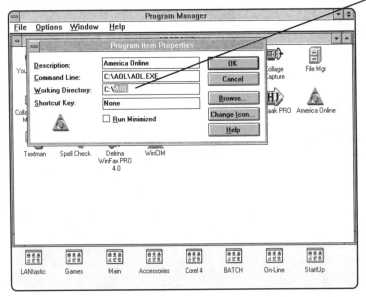

**5. Click** in the **Working Directory box** at the end of AOL.

**6. Press and hold** the **mouse button** and **drag** the cursor **over AOL** to highlight it.

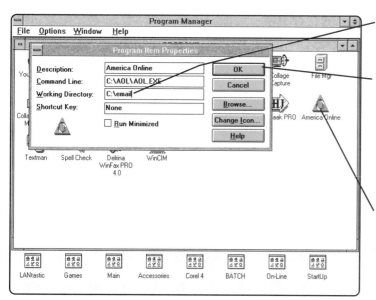

**7. Type email.** It will replace the highlighted text.

**8. Click** on **OK**. The dialog box will close.

You have to close America Online in order for this change to register.

**9. Click** on the **AOL icon**. America Online will appear full-size on your screen.

**10. Click twice** on the ⊟. A dialog box will appear asking if you are sure you want to sign off.

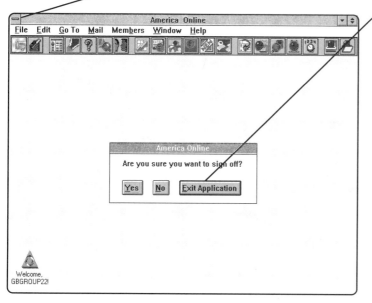

**11. Click** on **Exit Application**. America Online will close. From now on, it will always go to the e-mail directory when you save a letter.

# SENDING INTERNET MAIL TO YOUR REPRESENTATIVE

America Online has the Internet addresses of some interesting people. You can get the Internet addresses for the White House, NBC Nightly News, and some of the members of the United States Congress.

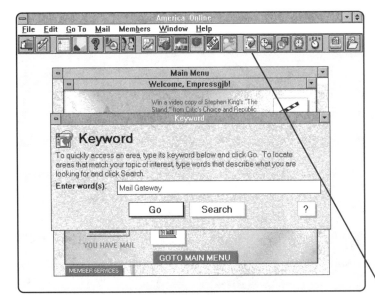

## Using a Keyword To Go to the Mail Gateway

You can click through layers of dialog boxes to get to the Mail Gateway, or you can use a keyword.

1. **Sign on** to America Online.

2. **Click** on the **Keyword icon** in the toolbar. It's the seventh one from the right. The Keyword dialog box you see here will appear.

3. **Type Mail Gateway** and **press Enter** (or click on Go). The Mail Gateway dialog box will appear.

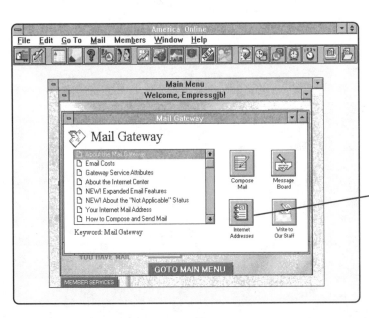

4. **Click** on the **Internet Addresses icon**. The Internet Addresses dialog box will appear.

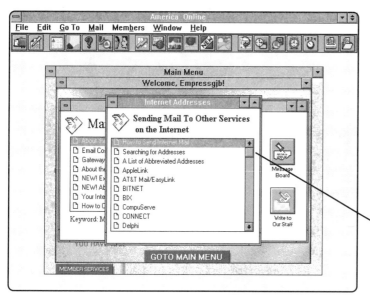

If you click twice on any of the documents in this dialog box, you'll get directions on how to address e-mail to a user of that particular on-line program.

There are more addresses in the bottom half of this dialog box.

5. **Click and hold** the **scroll button** and **drag** the button to the **bottom** of the scroll bar. This step will take you to the bottom of the list in this dialog box.

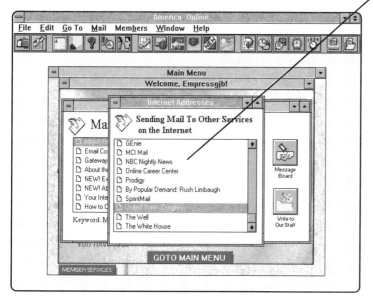

Notice the documents that contain the Internet addresses of NBC Nightly News, Rush Limbaugh, the United States Congress, and the White House.

6. **Click twice** on **any document** to open it on your screen.

We'll let you explore this section on your own. Have fun.

# Setting Up the Address Book

America Online's address book makes it easy to send Internet e-mail because it gives you a way to keep those long, complicated Internet addresses on file. In this chapter, you will do the following:

❖ Add Internet names and addresses to your address book
❖ Modify an address
❖ Delete an address
❖ Add a group address
❖ Use the address book to address an Internet e-mail letter

## ADDING NAMES AND ADDRESSES

You can open and edit the Address Book without being connected to America Online's computer. This means that you can do all your address book maintenance off-line at no charge!

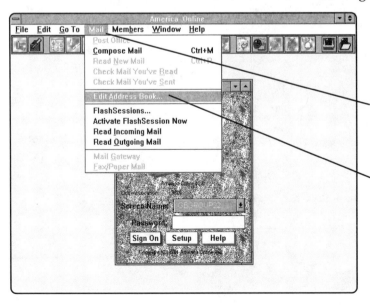

1. **Open America Online** if it is not already open, but don't sign on.

2. **Click** on **Mail** in the menu bar. A pull-down menu will appear.

3. **Click** on **Edit Address Book**. The Address Book dialog box will appear.

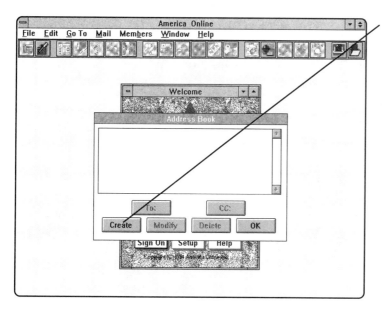

**4. Click** on **Create**. The Address Group dialog box will appear. The cursor will be flashing in the Group Name box.

**5. Type** the person's **name** and **press** the **Tab key** on your keyboard. The cursor will move to the Screen Names box.

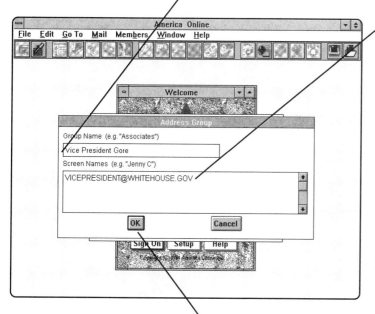

**6. Type** the person's **Internet address** here. (The Vice President's name should have a period between Vice and President. You're going to type it incorrectly here so that you can learn how to correct a name later in this chapter.) Internet names are not case sensitive, so it doesn't matter whether you type in all uppercase or lowercase letters or a combination of upper- and lowercase.

**7. Click** on **OK**. The Address Book dialog box will appear.

## Adding Another Name

**1. Repeat steps 4** through **6** in the previous section to add a second group name.

**2. Click** on **OK**. The Address Book dialog box will appear.

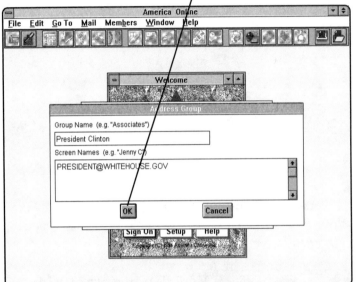

Notice that the names in the screen below are not in alphabetical order. *The AOL Address Book adds names only in order of entry.* The last name entered goes to the bottom of the list. For this reason, we keep our e-mail address list up-to-date in a Word table so that we can alphabetize the names automatically. Then, periodically, we delete most of the names from the AOL Address Book and reenter them in alphabetical order. (We hope that AOL will fix it so that you can sort the names in the address book!)

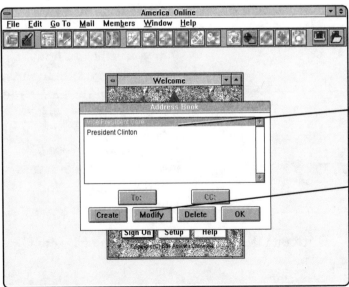

## EDITING AN ADDRESS

**1. Click** on the **name** of the person whose address you want **to edit**.

**2. Click** on **Modify**. The Address Group dialog box will appear. The cursor will be flashing in the Screen Name box.

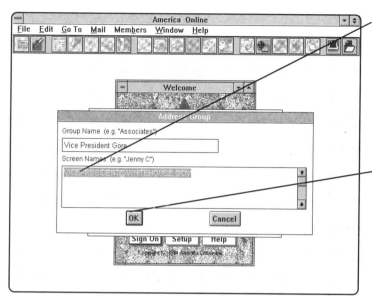

3. **Click twice** to **highlight** the **address**.

4. **Type** the **correct address**. In this example, there should be a period between VICE and PRESIDENT.

5. **Click** on **OK**. The Address Book dialog box will appear.

## DELETING AN ADDRESS

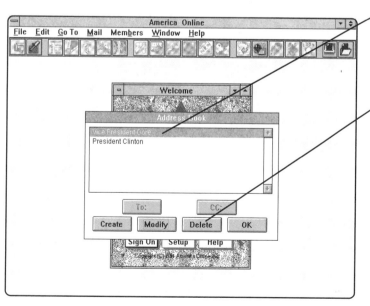

1. **Click** on the **name** of the person whose address you want **to delete** from your address book.

2. **Click** on **Delete**. The Delete dialog box will appear.

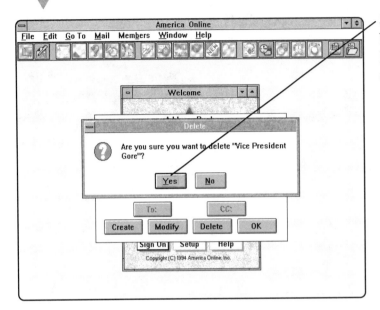

**3.** **Click** on **Yes**. The dialog box will disappear. (Republicans should love this one, eh?)

## ADDING A GROUP ADDRESS

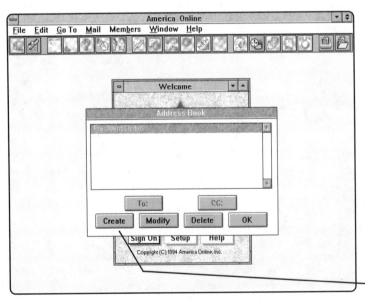

If you regularly send mail to the same group of people, you can create a group address and add the names of all appropriate people to the group. Thereafter, when you send mail to the group, a copy of the letter will automatically be sent to everyone in the group. If the address book is not already on your screen, repeat steps 2 and 3 on page 70.

**1.** **Click** on **Create**. The Address Group dialog box will appear. The cursor will be flashing in the Group Name box.

2. **Type** the **group name** (your choice) and **press** the **Tab key** on your keyboard. The cursor will move to the Screen Names box.

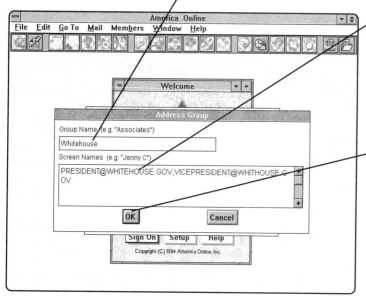

3. **Type** the **Internet address** of each person you want in the group. *Separate each address with a comma. Don't add a space before or after the comma.*

4. **Click** on **OK**. The Address Book dialog box will appear. You now have a group address. You use it just like a single address except that it addresses your letter to each member listed in the group.

## CLOSING THE ADDRESS BOOK

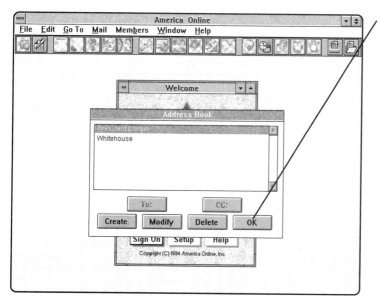

1. **Click** on **OK**. The Address Book dialog box will disappear.

## USING THE ADDRESS BOOK

You can use the Address Book to send an original letter or a carbon copy of the letter.

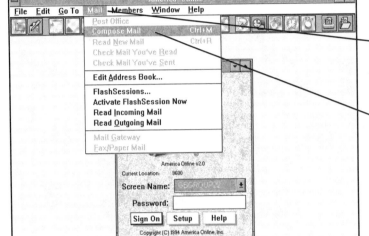

1. **Click** on **Mail** in the menu bar. A pull-down menu will appear.

2. **Click** on **Compose Mail**. The Compose Mail dialog box will appear.

3. **Click** on the **Address Book button**. The Address Book dialog box will appear.

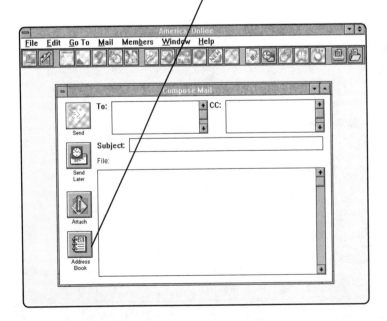

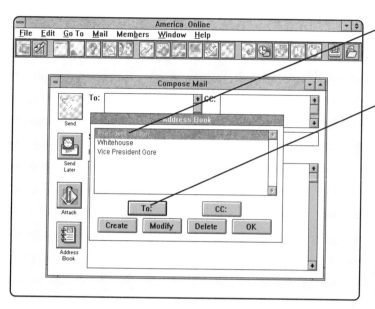

**4. Click** on the **name** of the person to whom you want to send an Internet letter.

**5. Click** on the **To button**. The Internet address you chose will appear in the To box of the Compose Mail dialog box.

**Note:** If you click on the group address, the results will be the same except that more than one address will appear in the To box.

Notice that the Internet address now appears in the To box (partially showing here).

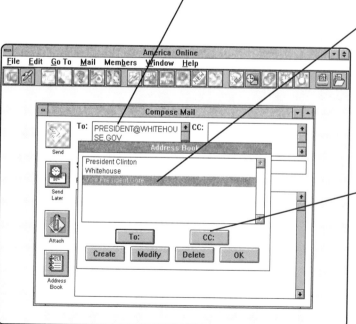

**6. Click** on the **name** of the person to whom you want **to send a copy** of this letter to highlight it. (Yes, we put Vice President Gore's Internet address back in our address book to keep the Democrats happy!)

**7. Click** on the **CC button**. The Internet address will appear in the CC box of the Compose Mail dialog box.

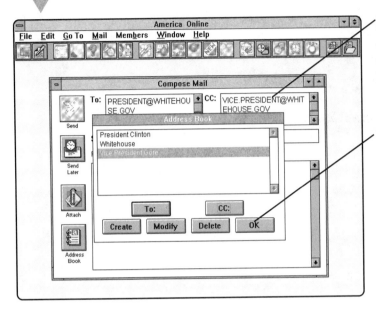

Notice that an Internet address now appears in the CC box (partially showing here) of the Compose Mail dialog box.

8. **Click** on **OK**. The Address Book dialog box will close and the Compose Mail dialog box will appear.

Notice that the Address Book has done its job!

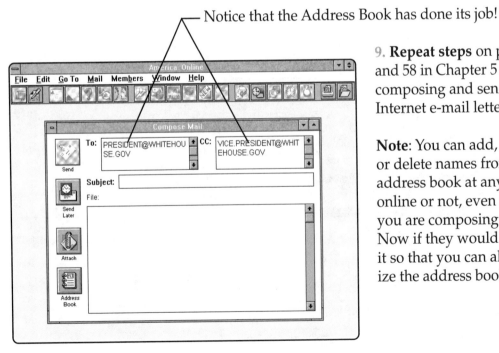

9. **Repeat steps** on pages 57 and 58 in Chapter 5 to finish composing and sending the Internet e-mail letter.

**Note**: You can add, modify, or delete names from the address book at any time, online or not, even when you are composing a letter. Now if they would only fix it so that you can alphabetize the address book names!

# Replying to and Forwarding Internet Mail

America Online automatically notifies you when you have mail. Once you're notified, reading, replying to, and forwarding Internet mail is quick and easy! In this chapter, you will do the following:

❖ Read mail
❖ Reply to and forward Internet mail
❖ Reread old mail and delete old mail
❖ Mark mail as "unread"
❖ Delete old mail
❖ Use the Post Office

## READING YOUR MAIL

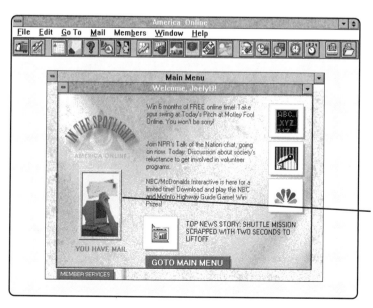

AOL lets you know as soon as you have mail.

1. **Open** and **log on** to America Online. If you have mail, you'll see a "letter" in the mailbox icon along with a message that you have mail.

2. **Click** on the **mailbox icon**. The New Mail dialog box will appear

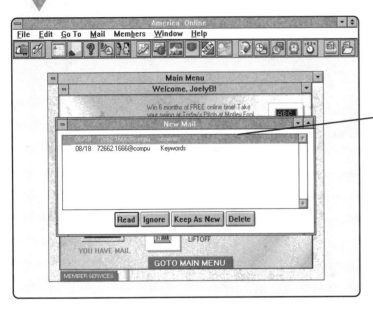

Each letter shows the date it was sent, the sender's address, and the subject of the letter.

**3. Click twice** on the **letter** you want **to read**. (You can also click once to highlight the letter and then click on the Read button.) The letter will appear on your screen.

## Viewing the Headers Information

Every letter sent through the Internet shows its route through the Internet, the sender, the recipient, the date, and the time at the bottom of the letter, in a section called "Headers."

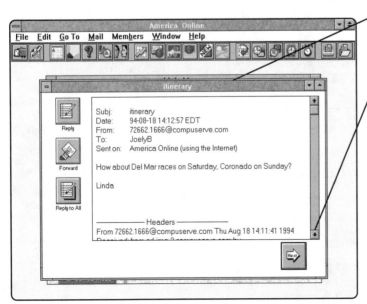

Notice that the subject of the letter appears in the title bar of the window.

**1. Click repeatedly** on the ⬇ to **scroll down** the letter. Eventually, depending on the length of the letter, the "headers file" will come into view. It shows you how the letter was routed along the information highway.

This is the Headers information, and it is inserted automatically when you send mail through the Internet. Aren't you glad you don't have to do it!

## PRINTING AND SAVING THE LETTER

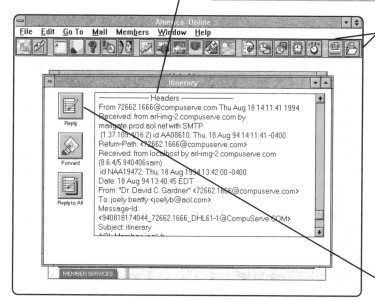

1. **Repeat** the **Printing and Saving steps** in Chapter 4 to print and/or save the letter.

## REPLYING TO AN INTERNET LETTER

The letter must be open on your screen to reply to it.

1. **Click** on **Reply.** An America Online dialog box will appear. The subject of the original letter will be in the title bar.

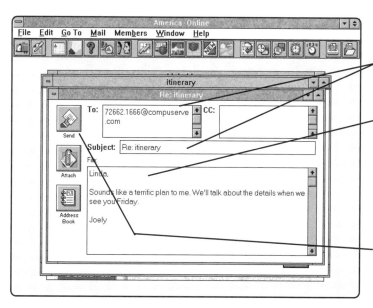

Notice that the address and subject are already filled in.

2. **Type** your **reply**. This is no different from sending a letter from scratch, except that the address and subject are already filled in for you.

3. **Click** on **Send.** An America Online dialog box will appear.

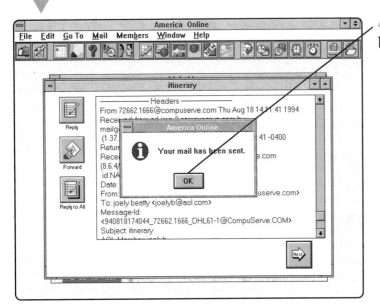

**4. Click** on **OK**. The dialog box will close.

## FORWARDING INTERNET MAIL

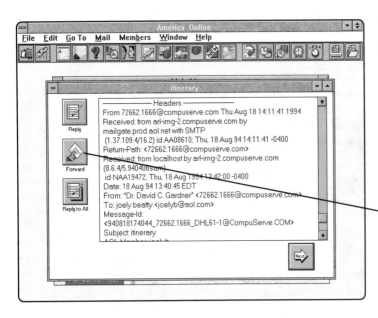

You can send any letter you receive to a third person. This is called *forwarding* mail. When you forward mail, you have to type a message to go with it. The letter you want to forward must be open on your screen.

**1. Click** on the **Forward button**. A mail dialog box will appear.

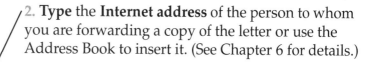

**2. Type** the **Internet address** of the person to whom you are forwarding a copy of the letter or use the Address Book to insert it. (See Chapter 6 for details.)

Notice that the title bar and the Subject box contain the letter's subject.

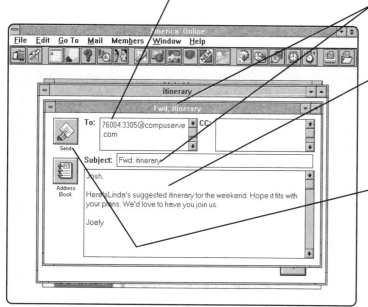

**3. Type** a **message**. Even though you are forwarding a letter, you must type a message here or it won't work!

**4. Click** on **Send**. An America Online dialog box will appear.

**5. Click** on **OK**. The dialog box will close. The letter has been forwarded.

The person who receives the forwarded letter in this example will receive *one* letter identified as "Fwd: itinerary" in his mailbox. The letter will have your message at the top of the letter and the forwarded message at the bottom of the letter.

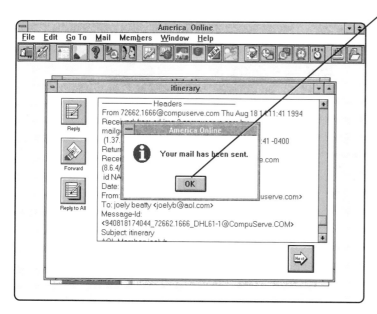

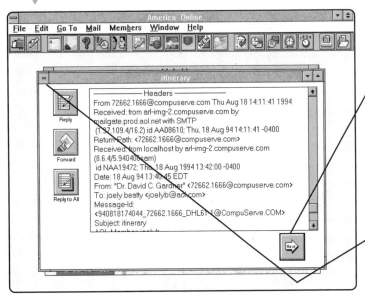

## READING THE NEXT LETTER

1. **Click** on **Next**. The next unread letter will appear.

2. **Repeat** the **steps** in the previous sections to print, save, reply to, or forward each letter.

3. When you finish with your mail, **click twice** on the **Control menu box (□)** on the left of the title bar to close this letter.

## KEEPING THE OLD AS "NEW"

You can mark a letter you have read to make it appear to the AOL computer to be new, unread mail. AOL will not delete *unread* mail until it is five weeks old, so you can use this option to hold a letter until you are ready to deal with it. If you are out of town, your secretary can screen your e-mail and mark specific letters "Keep As New." You can then deal with them when you return.

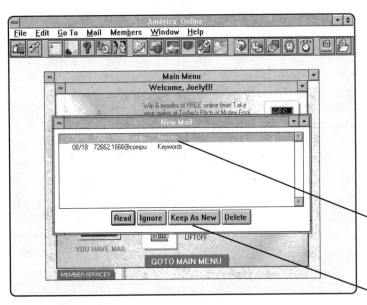

1. **Click** on the **letter** you want to keep as new to highlight it.

2. **Click** on **Keep As New**. A dialog box will appear.

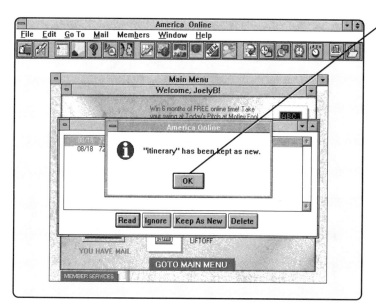

3. **Click** on **OK**. This letter will appear in the New Mail dialog box the next time you open it.

## DELETING MAIL YOU'VE READ

If you want to beat AOL to the punch and delete a letter yourself, it takes only a couple of clicks of the mouse.

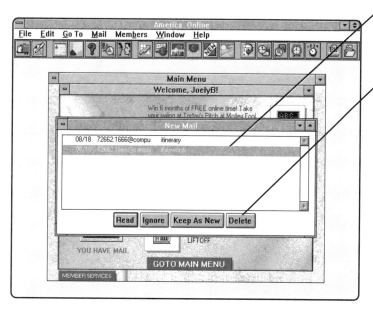

1. **Click** on the **letter** you want **to delete** to highlight it.

2. **Click** on the **Delete button**. An America Online dialog box will appear.

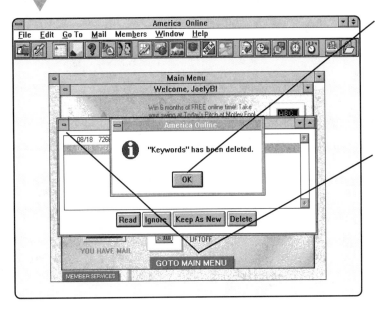

**3.** **Click** on **OK**. The dialog box will close. The letter will remain on the list until you close the mail dialog box. When you reopen it, the letter will be gone.

**4.** **Click twice** on the **Control menu box** (☐) on the right of the New Mail title bar to close the New Mail box. You'll be back at the Welcome screen.

## GOING TO THE POST OFFICE

There are lots of ways to get to your mail. So far in this chapter, you've been using the New Mail dialog box that appears when you click on the Mailbox icon in the Welcome screen. Using AOL's Post Office is another way to get to your mail.

**1.** **Click** on **GO TO MAIN MENU**. The Welcome screen will be sent to the background and the Main Menu will be brought to the foreground.

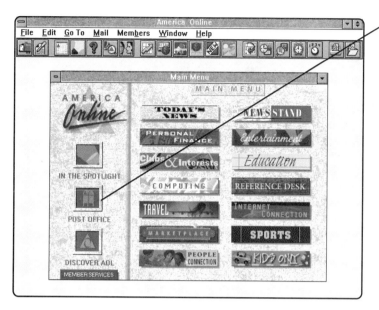

2. **Click** on **Post Office**. The Post Office dialog box will appear.

## READING OLD MAIL

America Online will automatically delete each letter you have read when it is seven days old. Until it is deleted, you can reread it, delete it yourself, or recode it to appear to AOL as unread (new) mail.

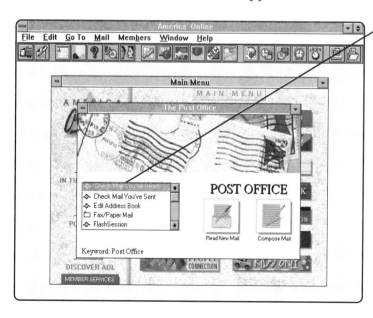

1. **Click twice** on the **Check Mail You've Read**. The Old Mail dialog box will appear with a list of all the letters you've read within the last week.

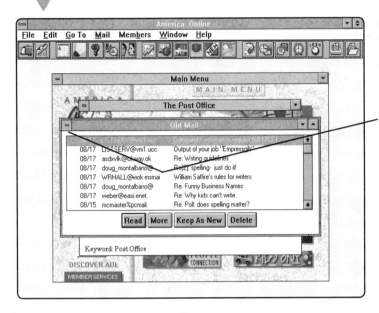

Once you're in this dialog box, you can read mail, mark it "Keep as New," or delete it.

2. To close this dialog box, **click twice** on the **Control menu box** (⊟) on the right of the Old Mail title bar. You'll be back at the Post Office.

## An Interesting Side Note...

Just a little aside before you close the Post Office. This has nothing to do with the Internet, but you can get the fax and phone numbers of members of the House of Representatives through the Post Office.

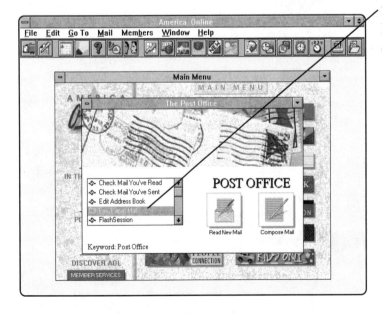

1. **Click twice** on **Fax/Paper Mail**. The Fax/Paper Mail dialog box will appear.

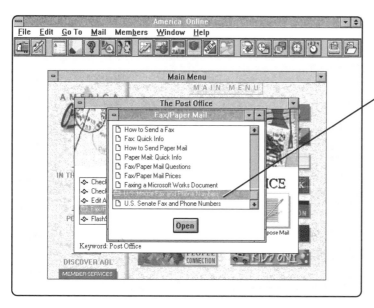

**2. Click** on ⬇ on the scroll bar until you can see the bottom of the list.

**3. Click twice** on **U.S. House Fax and Phone Numbers** or **U.S. Senate Fax & Phone Numbers** to open the document.

**4.** When you're through browsing, **close all open dialog boxes** until you're back at the Main Menu.

## USING A PULL-DOWN MENU TO SEE YOUR MAIL

One of the easiest ways, we think, to check mail you've read or sent is to use the Mail pull-down menu. This example shows the Main Menu in the background, but you can use the pull-down menu from anywhere in America Online.

**1. Click** on **Mail** in the menu bar. A pull-down menu will appear.

Notice that you can bypass the Post Office dialog box and click on Check Mail You've Read or Check Mail You've Sent.

# Using FlashSessions

If you send and receive a lot of mail, using America Online's FlashSession feature will save you much online time and money! It will send and receive your Internet and AOL mail and download AOL files automatically and then disconnect! You can then read your incoming mail off-line. You can also schedule FlashSessions to come on automatically when you are away from your computer or otherwise occupied. In this chapter, you will do the following:

❖ Set up your FlashSessions preferences
❖ Send mail, receive mail, and download files automatically
❖ Read your mail off-line
❖ Schedule a FlashSession

## OPENING FlashSessions FOR THE FIRST TIME

The first time you open FlashSessions, AOL walks you through a series of basic setup dialog boxes.

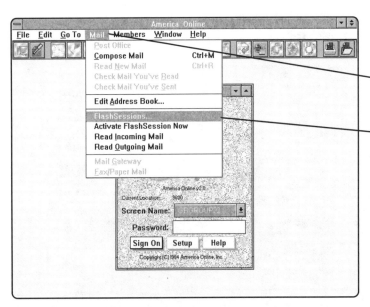

1. **Open America Online**, but don't sign on.

2. **Click** on **Mail**. A pull-down menu will appear.

3. **Click** on **FlashSessions**. A FlashSessions Walk-Through dialog box will appear.

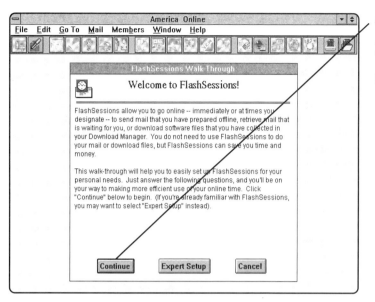

**4. Click** on **Continue**. Another FlashSession Walk-Through dialog box will appear.

## Setting Initial FlashSession Options

In this example, you will select the basic options for a FlashSession that sends mail, receives mail, and downloads attached files. In a later section, you will be able to change the options.

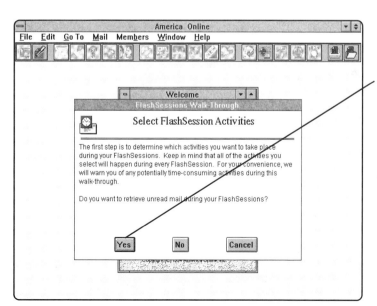

**1. Click** on **Yes**. Another FlashSession Walk-Through dialog box will appear.

*You have just set up FlashSessions to get your unread mail.*

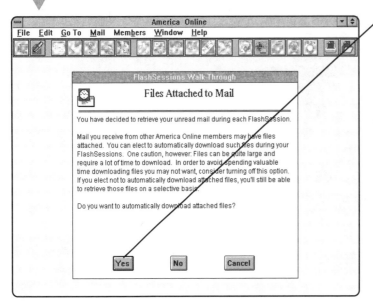

2. **Click** on **Yes**. Another FlashSession Walk-Through dialog box will appear.

*You have just set up FlashSessions to automatically download files attached to your incoming mail.*

At this writing, files can be attached only to AOL mail. You cannot attach files to Internet mail.

3. **Click** on **Yes**. Another FlashSession Walk-Through dialog box will appear.

*You have just set up FlashSessions to automatically send outgoing mail.*

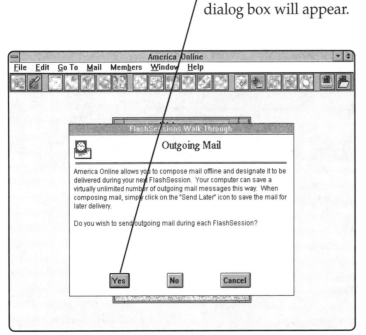

**4. Click** on **Yes**. Another FlashSession Walk-Through dialog box will appear.

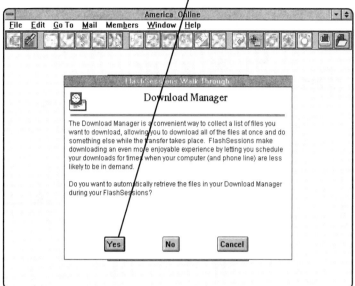

*You have just set up FlashSessions to automatically download files contained in your Download Manager.*

## SETTING UP FLASHSESSIONS FOR DIFFERENT SCREEN NAMES

If you have more than one AOL screen name, you can set FlashSessions to run for each screen name. AOL will connect and disconnect for each session in turn. However, in this section, you will set up FlashSessions to run with only one screen name.

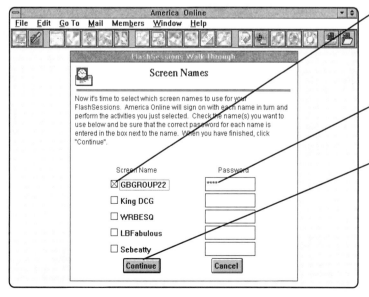

**1. Click** on the **screen name** of the one you want **to select** for a session to put an X in the box.

**2. Type** the **password** for the selected screen name.

**3. Click** on **Continue**. Another FlashSession Walk-Through dialog box will appear.

*You have just set up a screen name for a FlashSession.*

# FINISHING THE
# WALK-THROUGH SESSION

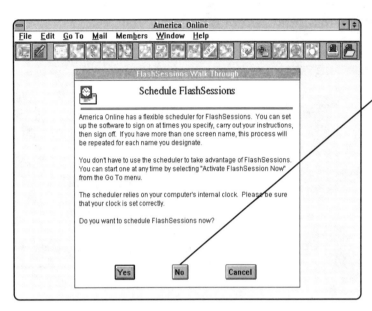

In this section, you will complete your first-time Walk-Through.

1. **Click** on **No**. Another FlashSessions Walk-Through dialog box will appear.

*You have just elected not to schedule a FlashSession at this time.* You will have an opportunity to do so later in this chapter.

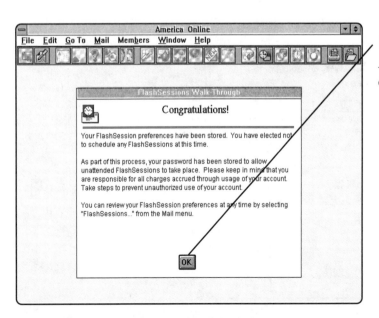

2. **Click** on **OK**. The America Online Welcome dialog box will reappear.

## SETTING UP A FlashSession

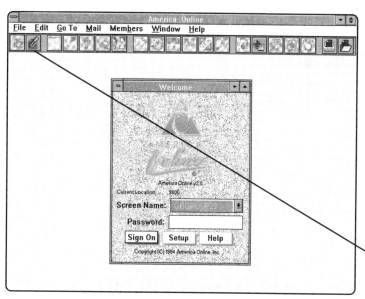

In the example in this section, you will both send mail and receive mail automatically. In addition, in this example, you will download a file attached to an e-mail letter.

### Composing Mail for a FlashSession

1. **Click** on the **Compose Mail icon** in the toolbar. The Compose Mail dialog box will appear.

2. **Compose** the **letter**. See Chapter 1 if you need help composing a letter.

**Note**: If you minimize the Compose Mail dialog box as you did in Chapter 1, the FlashSession will not send the letter.

3. **Click** on **Send Later**. An America Online dialog box will appear.

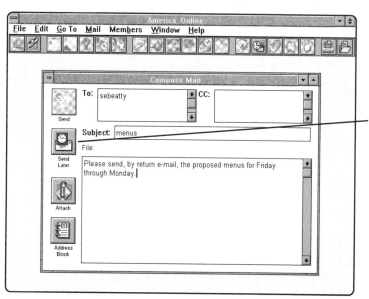

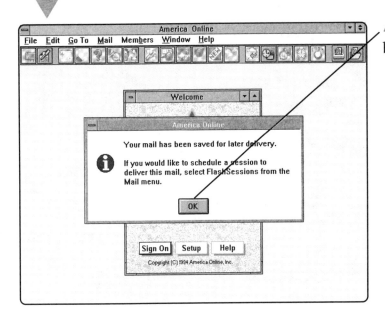

**4. Click** on **OK**. The dialog box will close.

## Changing Session Options

In the Walk-Through Session, you set up FlashSessions to perform all the basic options. In this section, you will change one of the options before beginning your first FlashSession.

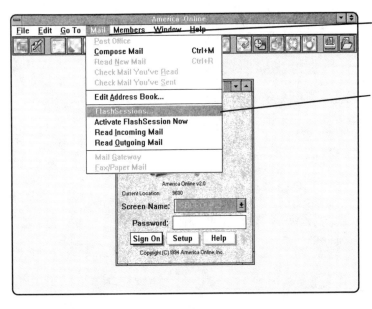

**1. Click** on **Mail** in the menu bar. A pull-down menu will appear.

**2. Click** on **FlashSessions**. The FlashSessions dialog box will appear.

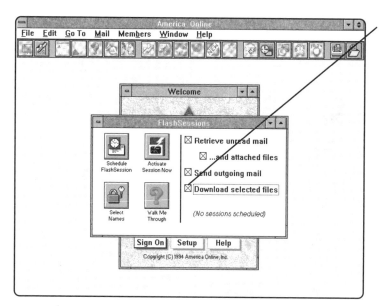

**3. Click** on **Download selected files** to *remove* the X from the box.

## RUNNING A FLASHSESSION

In this section, you will run your first FlashSession.

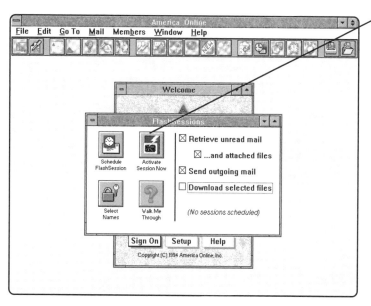

**1. Click** on the **Activate Session Now** icon. The Activate FlashSession Now dialog box will appear.

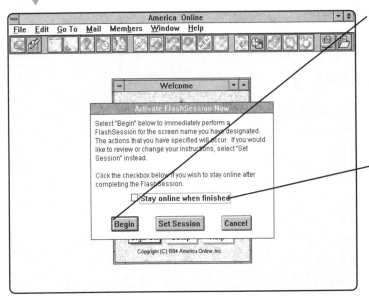

**2. Click** on **Begin**. America Online will begin the connection process. An America Online FlashSession Status dialog box will appear in the background.

❖ If you want to stay online after the FlashSession is finished, click on Stay online to put an ✕ in the box. *In this example, we did not choose to stay online.*

❖ Notice the dialog box. It will record every action taken in the FlashSession as each action occurs.

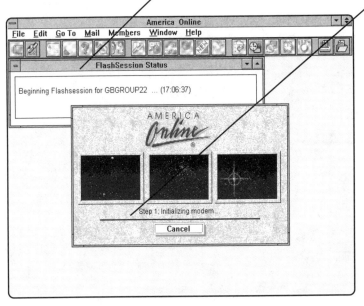

❖ AOL will go through the normal steps in the connecting process during a FlashSession.

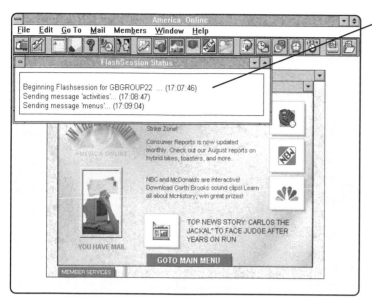

❖ While you are online, the status of the FlashSession is continually updated as AOL performs the tasks you have assigned to this session. Once the session is complete, AOL will disconnect automatically and the Goodbye America Online dialog box will appear. The FlashSession Status dialog box will appear behind it. It will contain a log of the session.

## READING THE FlashSession Log

You can review the FlashSession log to see if all the tasks were completed.

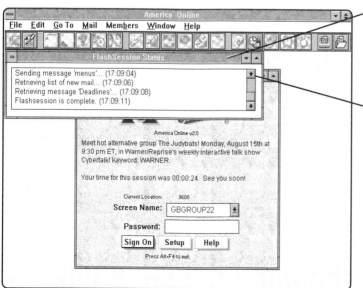

1. **Click** on the FlashSession Status title bar to bring the dialog box to the foreground, if necessary.

2. **Click** on the ⬆ or ⬇ to **scroll up or down** the log to review the results of your first FlashSession.

3. **Click twice** on the ⊟ in the left corner of the title bar to close the Status box.

# READING
# INCOMING MAIL OFF-LINE

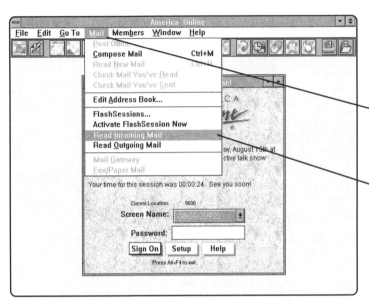

In this section, you will read, print, save, and delete the mail you just retrieved in your first FlashSession.

1. **Click** on **Mail** in the menu bar. A pull-down menu will appear.

2. **Click** on **Read Incoming Mail**. The Incoming FlashMail dialog box will appear.

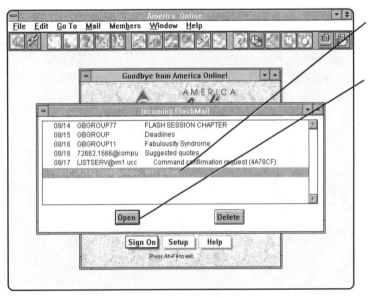

3. **Click** on the **letter** you want **to open** to highlight it.

4. **Click** on **Open**. The letter will open.

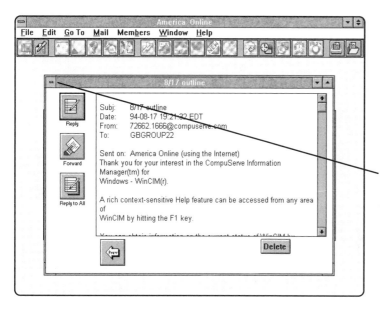

You can save or print the e-mail letter by using the Save and Print icons. If you need help printing or saving a file, see Chapter 1, the sections on printing and saving files.

5. **Click twice** on the ▭ in the left corner of the title bar to close the letter.

## Deleting and Closing

1. **Click** on the **letter** you want **to delete** to highlight it.

2. **Click** on **Delete**. An America Online dialog box will appear.

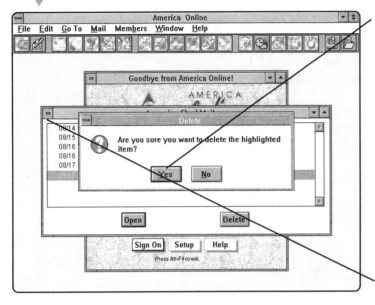

**3. Click** on **Yes**. The dialog box will close, and the file will be deleted from the Incoming FlashSession dialog box.

**Note:** Even though you have deleted the file from the Incoming FlashSession dialog box, the original file will remain in your Old Mail dialog box when next you go back online.

**4. Click twice** on the **Control menu box** (▭) in the left corner of the title bar to close the dialog box.

## SCHEDULING A SESSION

You can set up AOL to run a FlashSession at specific times on specific days for one or more of your screen names. In this section, you will set up AOL to run FlashSessions once a day on Monday through Thursday at 11 p.m.

**1. Repeat steps 2 and 3** on page 90 to open the FlashSessions dialog box shown here.

**2. Click** on **Schedule FlashSession**. The Schedule FlashSessions dialog box will appear.

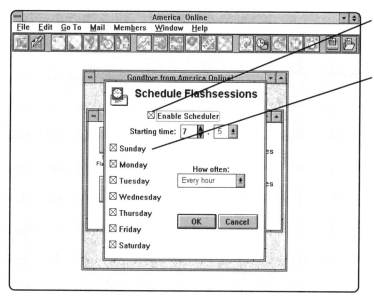

3. **Click** on **Enable Scheduler** to put an X in the box.

4. **Click** on the **days** you do *not* want to run a FlashSession to remove the Xs from the box.

5. **Click repeatedly** on the ⬆ to the right of the Starting Time box until 23 appears in the box.

6. **Click** on the ⬇ to the right of the How Often box. A drop-down list will appear.

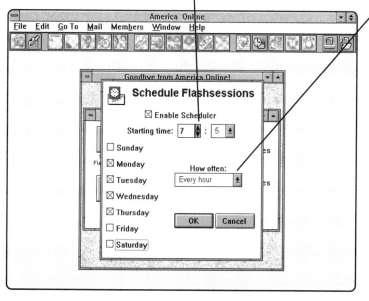

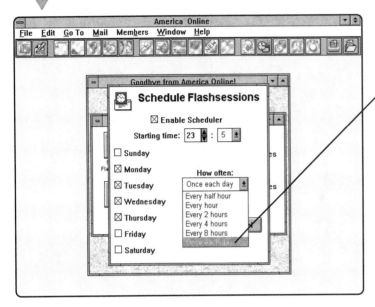

**Note**: In military time, 23 (2300 hours) is 11 p.m.

7. **Click** on **Once each day**. The drop-down list will close, and "Once each day" will appear in the box.

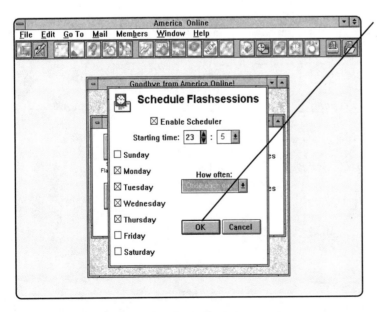

8. **Click** on **OK**. The dialog box will close.

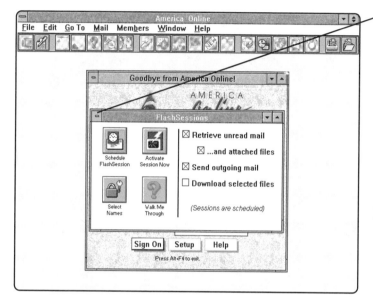

**9. Click twice** on the ⊟ in the left corner of the FlashSessions dialog box. The dialog box will close.

You have just scheduled a FlashSession. In order for the scheduled session to work, you must leave your computer turned on and America Online booted up but not signed on.

# Checking Spelling

Our first trauma when sending Internet e-mail was finding that America Online doesn't have a Spell Check program. Egad, what now? At first we used our word-processing program to compose e-mail and then used the Windows Clipboard to copy and paste the text into America Online's Compose Mail window. This method turned out to be such a colossal pain in the neck that we skipped spell-checking altogether. Then one day we found Next Generation Software's Spell Check program. Yours for the asking! In this chapter, you will do the following:

❖ Download Spell Check from AOL to your computer
❖ Set up Spell Check
❖ Check the spelling of an e-mail letter

## GETTING SPELL CHECK

Spell Check is a shareware program. This means that you can get a review copy through America Online, try it, and if you like it, send a modest fee to the developer for a registered copy. In this section, you will download a copy of Spell Check.

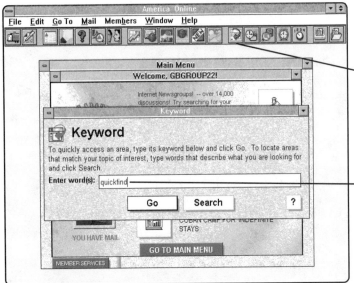

1. **Sign on to America Online**.

2. **Click** on the **Keyword button** on the toolbar. The Keyword dialog box will appear. It's the seventh icon from the right.

3. **Type quickfind** and **click** on **Go**. The File Search dialog box will appear.

4. **Type wcspell3.zip**.

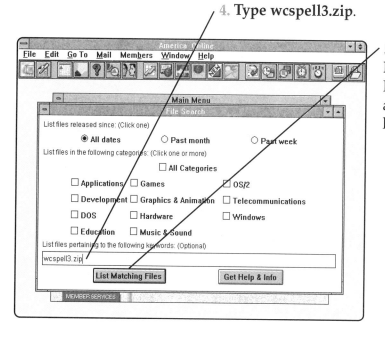

5. **Click** on **List Matching Files**. The File Search Results dialog box will appear with the file highlighted.

6. **Click** on **Download Now.** The Download Manager dialog box will appear.

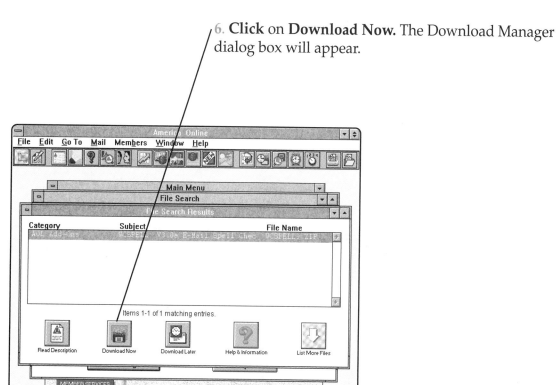

**7.** **Click twice** on **c:\** in the Directories box. AOL will not only automatically download and unzip (decompress) the files for Spell-Check but also make a *subdirectory* ("c:\wcspell3") that will contain all the Spell Check files.

**8.** **Click** on **OK**. The File Transfer dialog box will appear.

**9.** **Click** on **Sign Off After Transfer** to put an ✕ in the box. It will take about eight minutes to complete. Then, after the file is transferred, the Goodbye America Online dialog box will appear. A message box about extracting files will flash by so fast that you can hardly read it, and you will be disconnected from AOL.

**Note**: In the normal course of events, "Sign Off After Transfer" when downloading a file is optional. However, if you are going to follow along in this chapter, please elect to do so now.

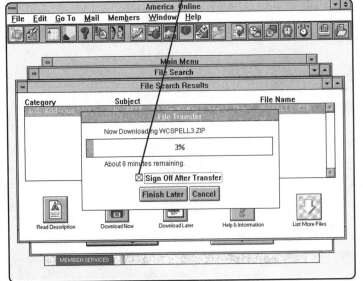

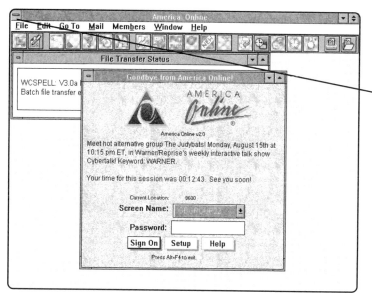

## CLOSING AMERICA ONLINE

**1. Click twice** on the **Control menu box** (☐) in the left corner of the title bar. America Online will close.

## CREATING THE SPELL CHECK ICON

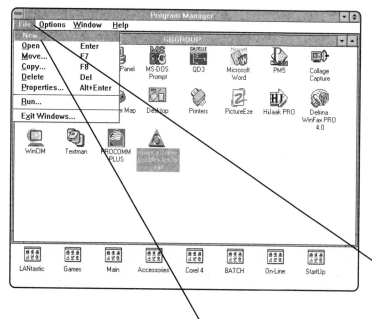

In this section, you will create an icon for Spell Check. You'll even create a shortcut key so that you can call up the Spell Check program with a simple keystroke combination.

**1. Open** the group window where you want to put the icon. In this example, it is GBGroup.

**2. Click** on **File** in the menu bar. A pull-down menu will appear.

**3. Click** on **New**. The New Program Object dialog box will appear.

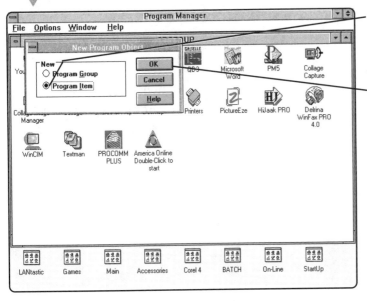

**4.** **Click** on **Program Item** if it doesn't already have a dot in the circle.

**5.** **Click** on **OK**. The Program Item Properties dialog box will appear. The cursor will be flashing in the Description box.

**6.** **Type Spell Check** and **press** the **Tab key**. The cursor will move to the Command Line box.

**7.** **Type c:\wcspell3\wcspell3** in the Command Line box and **press** the **Tab key. Type c:\wcspell** in the Working Directory box.

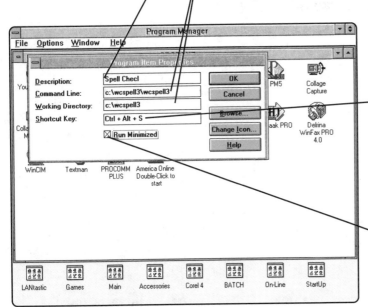

**8.** **Press** the **Tab key** to move to the Shortcut Key box.

**9.** **Type s** in the Shortcut Key box. You don't have to highlight "None" before you type "s." Ctrl+Alt+S will automatically replace None.

**10.** **Click** on **Run Minimized** to put an ✕ in the box

**11.** **Click** on **OK**. The dialog box will close.

## OPENING SPELL CHECK
## FOR THE FIRST TIME

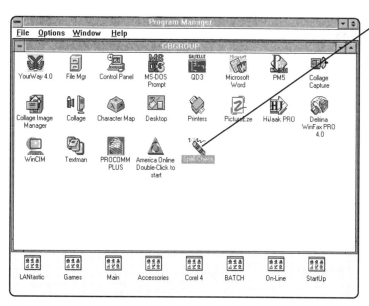

1. **Click twice** on the **Spell Check icon**. A Spell Check Setup dialog box will appear.

**Note**: If you get an error message that reads "Cannot find VBRUN300.DLL," you will have to download it from AOL and put it in your c:\windows\system directory. In this case, click on Close in the message box. Another "Cannot find..." message box will appear. Click on OK. Next, repeat steps 2 through 8 in the "Getting Spell Check" section at the beginning of this chapter to download vbrun300.dll (Runtime Module.) After it's downloaded, use File Manager to copy it to your windows\ system directory. If you need help with this process, send an e-mail message to Next Generation Software. They will help you solve the problem. Their screen name is NEXTGENSFT.

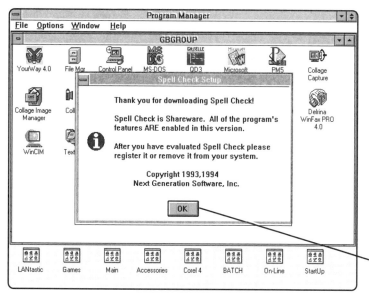

2. **Click** on **OK**. Another Spell Check Setup dialog box will appear.

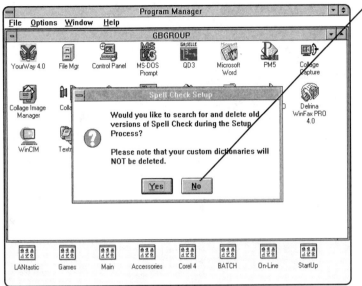

3. **Click** on **No** unless you have a previous version installed. Another Spell Check dialog box will appear.

## Attaching the Word for Windows Custom Dictionary

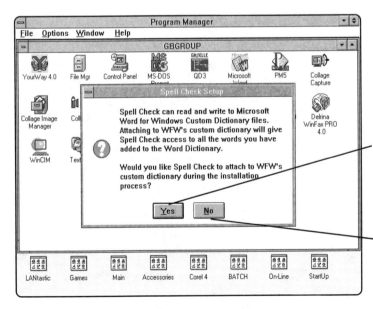

If you are using Word2 or Word6 as your word-processing program, you can attach your current custom dictionary to the Spell Check dictionary.

1. **Click** on **Yes** if you have Word2 or Word6.

**OR**

**Click** on **No** if you have another word-processing program.

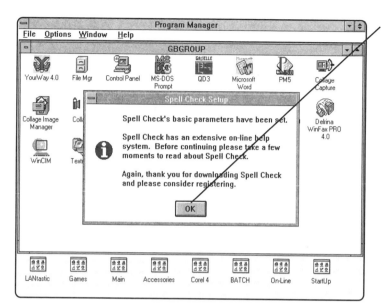

**2. Click OK.** A Quick Introduction to Spell Check 3.0 window will appear.

## Printing Help Topics

Your window may be a different size than the one you see in this example.

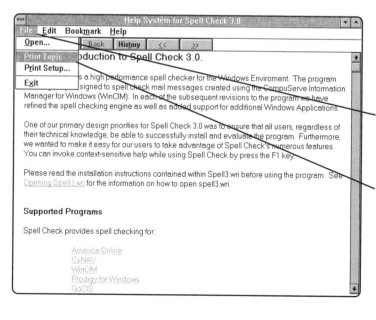

You can learn the names of the programs for which Spell Check provides spell-checking by printing the current topic screen.

**1. Click** on **File** in the menu bar. A pull-down menu will appear.

**2. Click** on **Print Topic.** You'll see a Print message box, and then the "Quick Introduction" page will print.

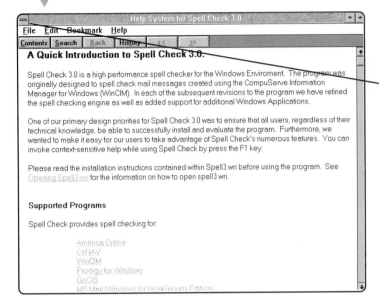

## Closing the Help Window

**1. Click twice** on the **Control menu box** (⊟) on the left of the menu bar to close the Help window.

## Setting Up a Closing Option

If you like to add a specific closing, such as your name and Internet address, to your e-mail, you can set up Spell Check to add a customized closing every time it checks your spelling.

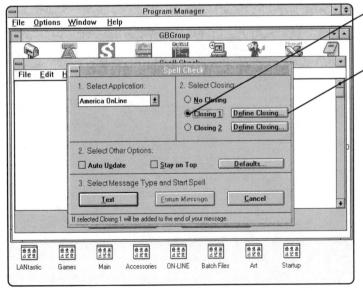

**1. Click** on **Closing 1** to put a dot in the circle.

**2. Click** on the **Define Closing button** to the right of Closing 1. The Define Closing 1 dialog box will appear.

3. **Type** the **first line** of your own **customized closing and press** the **Tab key**. The cursor will move to the next line.

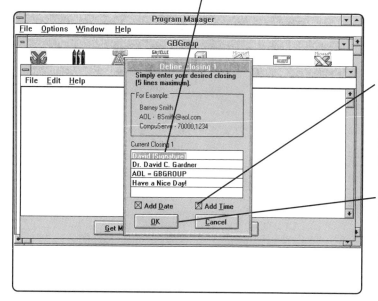

4. **Repeat step 3** for each line of the closing.

**Note:** You can also add the date and time to your closing by clicking on the respective boxes to put an ✕ in the box.

5. **Click** on **OK.** Another Define Closing 1 dialog box will appear.

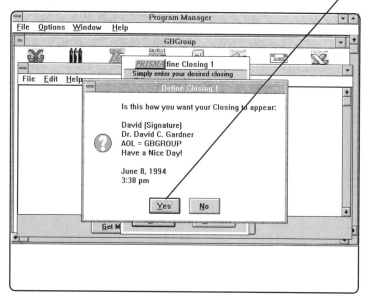

6. **Click** on **Yes if** the closing is **correct**. The Spell Check dialog box will appear. **If** the closing is **not correct, click** on **No**. The previous dialog box will reappear. You can make corrections by repeating steps 3 through 5.

7. **Repeat steps 1 through 6** if you want to create Closing 2. (For example, Closing 1 might be a personal closing, and Closing 2 might be a more formal business closing.)

# Fine-Tuning Spell Check

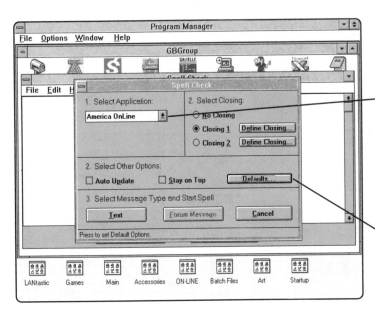

In this section, you will set up Spell Check to work the way you want.

**1.** If America Online doesn't appear in the Select Application box, **click** on the ⬇ **to open** a list of applications. Scroll up to America Online and click.

**2. Click** on **Defaults.** A Spell Check Default Settings dialog box will appear.

**3. Click** on **Run Spell Check Minimized** to put an ✕ in the box. Spell Check will run minimized in the background when you open it.

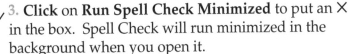

**4. Click** on **Automatically Update When Spell Check Complete** to put an ✕ in the box if it is not already there. Spell Check will now automatically return to AOL and update your letter upon completion of the spell-check.

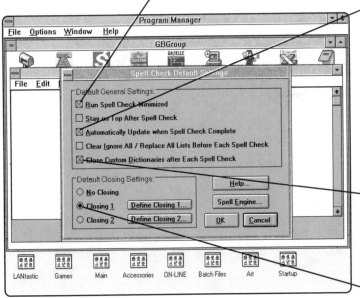

Notice that Close Custom Dictionaries after Each Spell Check already has an ✕ in the box.

**5. Click** on **Closing 1** (or the closing you prefer to have as your default closing) to put a dot in the circle.

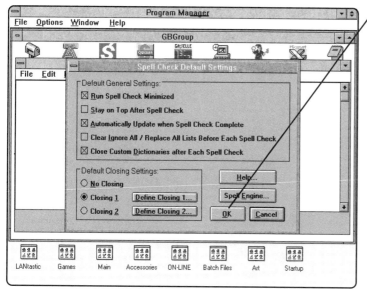

6. **Click** on **OK**. The original Spell Check dialog box will reappear.

**Note:** Once you have selected the options in the Spell Check Default Settings dialog box, they will remain in effect until you change them. You can change them by clicking on Edit in the menu bar and then clicking on Defaults. This will open the Default Settings dialog box you see here.

## CLOSING SPELL CHECK

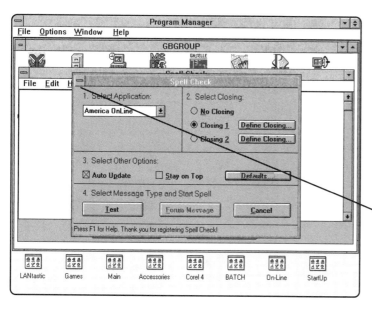

You will close Spell Check now so that in the next section you can see what the process of opening Spell Check and AOL will be like. In the section that follows, you will learn to use Spell Check to check the spelling of your AOL Internet e-mail.

1. **Click twice** on the **Control menu box** (☐) in the left corner of the title bar to close the dialog box. The Spell Check window will move to the foreground.

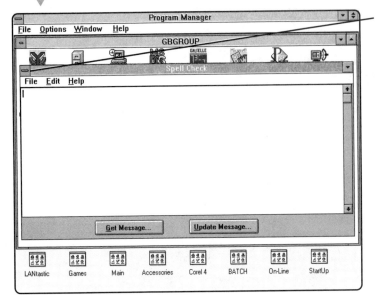

2. **Click twice** on the **Control menu box** (☐) on the left of the Spell Check window title bar. Spell Check will close.

**Note**: If you do not have a registered copy, the Registration Information dialog box will appear. Click on No. You will get a chance to register your copy in the last section of this chapter, entitled "Registering Spell Check."

## USING SPELL CHECK

Spell Check should be open and running in the background when you are using it with America Online. It's just easier that way.

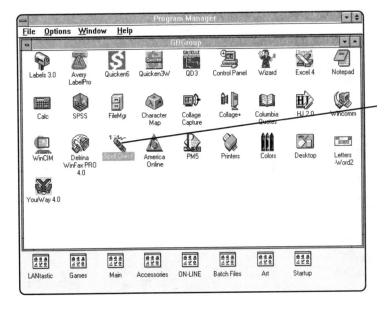

## Opening Spell Check in the Background

1. **Click twice** on the **Spell Check program icon**. It may appear as an icon at the bottom of your screen. If you have Program Manager maximized, your screen will flicker a little, but you won't see any change in your screen. However, Spell Check is now running in the background, waiting for your call!

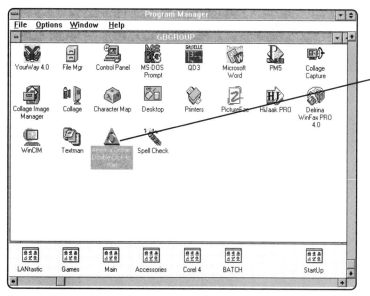

## Opening AOL Compose Mail

1. **Click twice** on the **America Online program icon**. The America Online Sign On window will appear.

2. **Click** on **Mail** in the menu bar. A pull-down menu will appear.

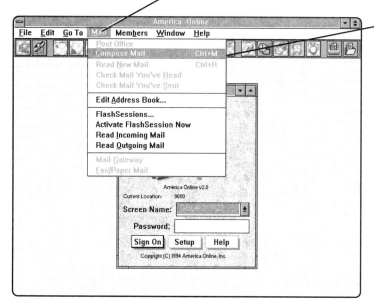

3. **Click** on **Compose Mail**. The Compose Mail dialog box will appear.

## Composing the Letter

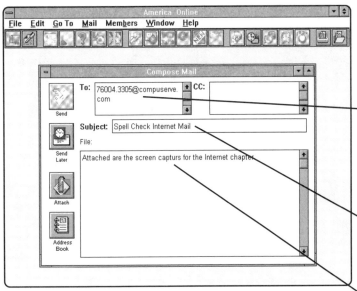

In the following example, we have purposely misspelled a word so we can show you Spell Check in action.

1. **Type** a **mailing address** and **press** the **Tab key twice** on your keyboard. The cursor will move to the Subject box.

2. **Type** a **subject** and **press** the **Tab key**. The cursor will move to the text box.

3. **Type** the **message**. Notice the misspelled word: "capturs."

## Starting Spell Check

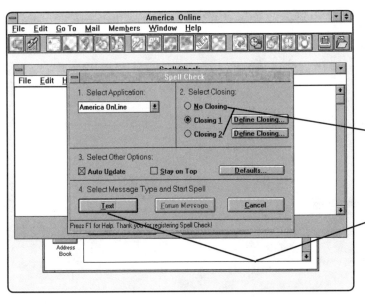

1. **Press and hold** the **Ctrl** and **Alt keys** and **type** the letter **s** (Ctrl+Alt+s). The Spell Check dialog box you see here will appear.

2. If you don't want to use Closing 1 for this letter, **click** on **Closing 2** or **No Closing**.

3. **Click** on the **Text button**. Another Spell Check dialog box will appear with the first misspelled or unrecognized word.

## Correcting Misspelled Words

1. **Click** on the **correctly spelled word**. In this example, the correct word is "captures."

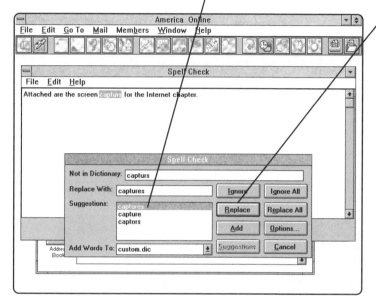

2. **Click** on **Replace**. Spell Check will highlight the next word.

## Adding a Word to the Custom Dictionary

A spell-check dictionary can't spell. No kidding. It can only check to see if a word in your text matches a word in the dictionary. Because we'll be using the word Internet frequently, we'll add it to our dictionary in this example.

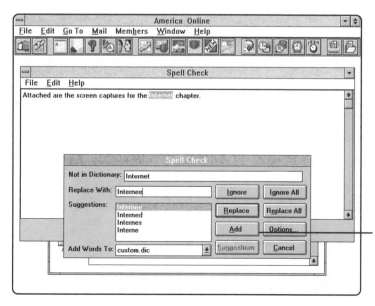

1. **Click** on **Add**. "Internet" will be added to your dictionary.

Notice that the Closing you set up previously has automatically been added to the bottom of your letter. (If you make changes to your letter and spell-check it again, the closing will be added again. Just delete the second closing.)

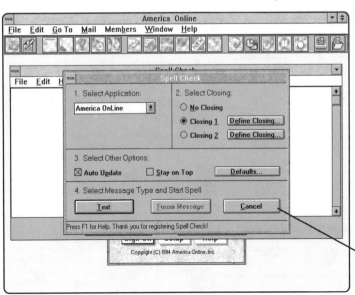

If you copied this message to learn how to use Spell Check, **click twice** on the **Control menu box** (▤) on the left of the Compose Mail title bar to close the dialog box. An AOL dialog box will appear.

2. **Click** on **No**.

## Registering Spell Check

You can register now or you can skip this section for the moment, work with the program, and register later if you like it. If you decide to use Spell Check, make certain that you pay for a registered copy. It's only fair.

1. **Press** and **hold** the **Ctrl** and **Alt keys** on your keyboard and **type** the letter **s** (Ctrl+Alt+s). The Spell Check dialog box will appear.

2. **Click** on **Cancel.** The dialog box will close.

**3. Click** on **File** on the menu bar. A pull-down menu will appear.

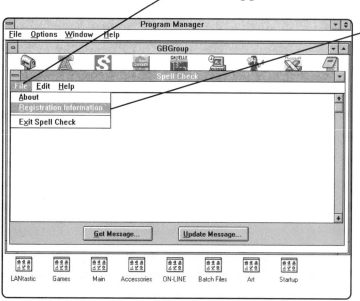

**4. Click** on **Registration Information**. The Register dialog box will appear.

**5. Click** on **Yes** to print an order form. Once it's printed, fill it out and mail your check today. Shortly thereafter, you will receive a registered copy on disk and a manual.

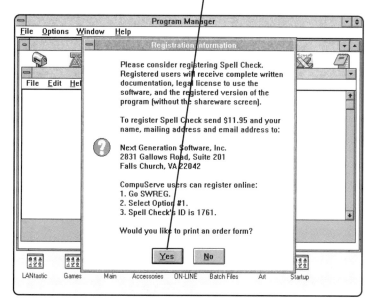

Converting the "trial copy" you just downloaded to a registered copy is very easy. Instructions come with the registered copy.

**6. Repeat step 2** in the section entitled "Closing Spell Check," earlier in this chapter to close.

**PART III: JOINING INTERNET DISCUSSION GROUPS**

**CHAPTER**

# Joining an Internet Mailing List

An Internet mailing list is a discussion group on a specific topic. There are thousands of mailing lists on all sorts of topics. Some are just for fun, and some are professional. Members send in letters to suggest topics for discussion, respond to other members' comments, and ask for help or advice. If your reply is of general interest, you can respond to the entire membership or you can send a personal letter to an individual member. You, as a member of the list, get all the general mail delivered to your mailbox. Some mailing lists generate considerable mail, so we suggest, you consider creating a special screen name for your mailing lists so that the mail doesn't get mixed up with your regular correspondence. In this chapter, you will do the following:

❖ Create a new screen name for mailing lists
❖ Search for and join a mailing list

## CREATING A SCREEN NAME FOR MAILING LISTS

Mailing lists can generate a great deal of mail. David belongs to a few that generate 2MB worth of mail a week. One way to deal with this is to create a separate screen name and to subscribe to the lists under that name. We'll teach you a neat trick for managing your mailing-list mail in Chapter 11, but it is based on having a separate screen name. If you don't want to do this, however, simply skip this.

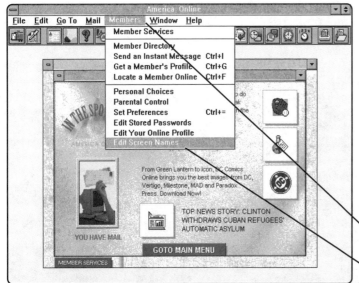

1. **Click** on **Members**.

2. **Click** on **Edit Screen Names**.

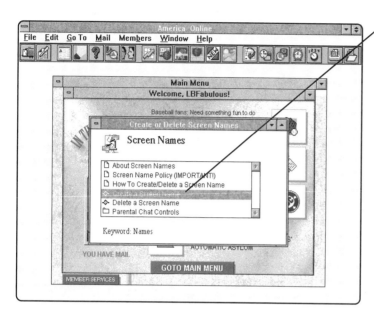

**3. Click twice** on **Create a Screen Name**. The Create a Screen Name dialog box will open.

**4. Repeat steps 4 through 8** starting on page 20 to create a screen name for your mailing lists.

After you create the name, you'll have to sign off from your current name, switch to the new name, and sign on again under the new screen name.

## SEARCHING FOR A MAILING LIST

After you are signed on, you can use the Internet Connection through the Main Menu to begin your search.

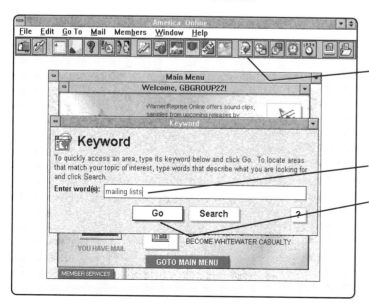

**OR**

**1. Click** on the **Keyword icon** in the menu bar. It's the seventh from the right. A dialog box will appear.

**2. Type mailing lists**.

**3. Click** on **Go** (or press Enter). The Internet Mailing Lists window will appear.

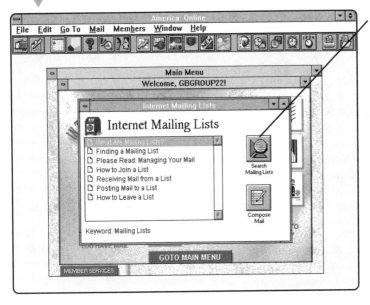

**4. Click** on **Search Mailing Lists**. The Internet Mailing Lists dialog box will appear.

There are literally thousands of mailing lists from which to choose. There are mailing lists devoted to such diverse topics as New Orleans, individual musicians or rock groups, alternative lifestyles, Polish and Irish culture, computer programming languages, prenatal care, and windsurfing. There are mailing lists that are strictly for fun and others that are professional in nature. You can search for a mailing list right on your computer.

5. **Type** the **topic** in which you are interested. In this example, it is communication.

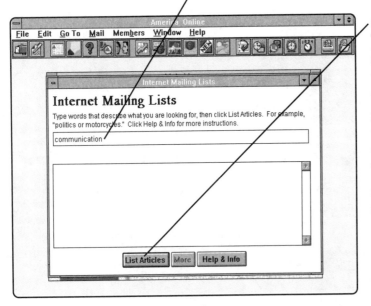

6. **Click** on **List Articles**. The computer will display all Mailing Lists that have "communication" in the title. It will also display all mailing lists that have "communication" anywhere in the description. This can produce some seemingly off-the-wall matches. However, if you scroll through the description of the mailing list, somewhere in the description will be the word you typed to begin your search.

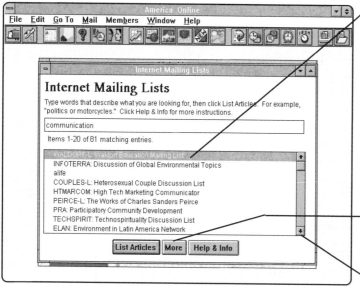

Notice that this first screen contains only 20 of 81 matches that the computer found at this time. It's possible that listings will have been added (or deleted) at the time of your search, so the total number of entries may be more or less than 81.

6. **Click** on **More** to add the remaining items to the list.

7. **Click** on the ⬇ on the scroll bar **to scroll** through the list.

## VIEWING A DESCRIPTION OF A MAILING LIST

If a particular listing arouses your curiosity, you can see a description of the mailing list.

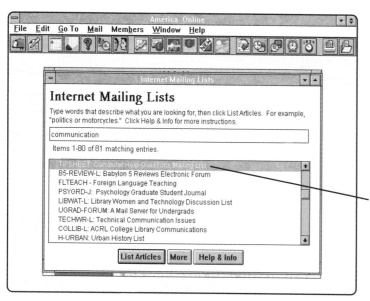

1. **Click twice** on the **topic** of interest. In this example, it is TIPSHEET. The description page will appear on your screen.

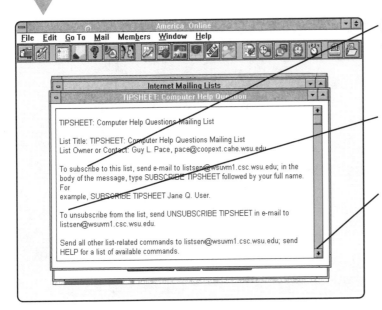

Notice that the description contains directions on how to subscribe to, or join, the mailing list.

It also contains directions on how to unsubscribe from, or leave, the list.

2. **Click** on the ⬇ on the scroll bar **to scroll** through the document.

## PRINTING A DESCRIPTION OF A MAILING LIST

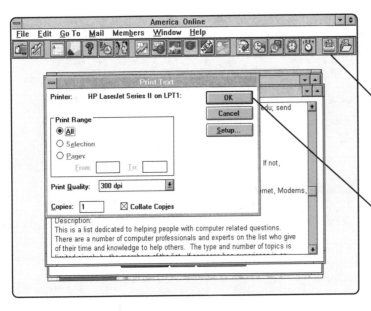

If you're interested in a mailing list, print the description.

1. **Click** on the **Print icon** in the toolbar while the description of the mailing list is on your screen. The Print dialog box will appear.

2. **Click** on **OK**. The page will print.

If you want to join this list, file the printed copy. It contains directions on how to join and leave the list. Or you can save the letter on your hard drive.

## RECEIVING A DIGEST OF ARTICLES

Some mailing lists offer the option of receiving a digest, which is a single file containing all the letters posted to the mailing list on a daily or weekly basis.

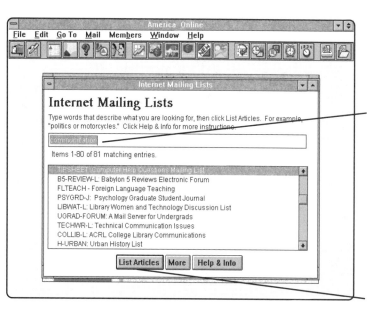

Notice that instructions for receiving a digest are included in the mailing list description.

**1. Click twice** on the **Control menu box** (⊟) on the left of the description title bar to close the window.

## SEARCHING FOR MORE LISTS

You can search for related topics or a completely new topic by changing the search word.

**1. Click twice** in the search word box. The word will be highlighted.

**2. Type** the **new search word**. It will replace the highlighted word. In this example, the new word is "technical."

**3. Click** on **List Articles**.

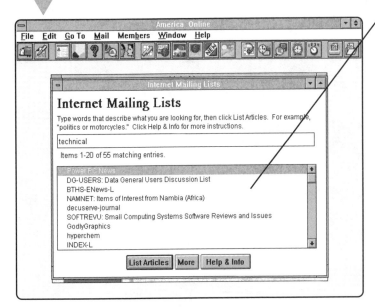

A new selection of mailing lists will appear.

## REFINING YOUR SEARCH WITH "AND," "OR," AND "BUT NOT"

You can use specific words to expand or limit the number of possible matches.

**1. Type technical and communication** in the search word box to limit the search to topics that include *both* words in the name or description.

**2. Click** on **List Articles**. As you can see, this resulted in six matches at the time of our search.

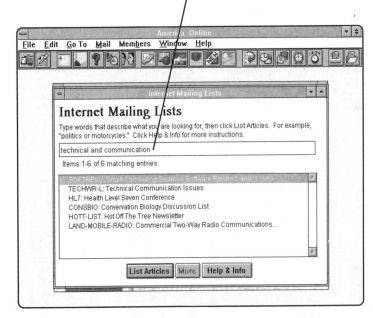

Use *or* to expand the search. For example, type *technical or communication* in the search word box for a list of topics that have *either* technical *or* communication in the name or description. When we did this search, it resulted in 130 matches.

Type *communication but not technical* for a list of all communication topics that do not include the word "technical" in the name or description. This resulted in 21 matches when we did it.

## JOINING A MAILING LIST

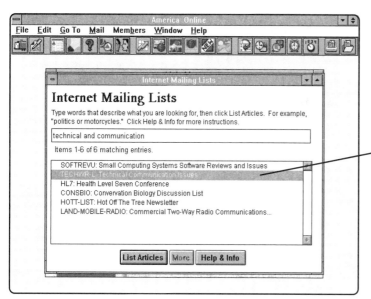

Joining a mailing list is very easy. This section will show you how to join a mailing list by using the Technical Communications mailing list as an example.

1. After you find a mailing list you would like to join, **click twice** on the **name**. The description of the mailing list will appear.

## Copying and Pasting the Subscription Address

All mailing lists have one address for subscriptions and another address for correspondence. It's important not to get them confused. You can copy and paste the subscription address into your request so that there is no chance for error.

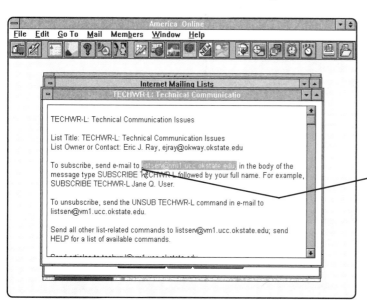

1. **Place** the **mouse arrow** on the **first letter** of the subscription address **and click twice**. The address will be highlighted.

2. **Click** on **Edit** in the menu bar. A pull-down menu will appear.

3. **Click** on **Copy**. You won't see any change in your screen, but the high-lighted address is now copied to the Clipboard, an electronic storage area on your computer.

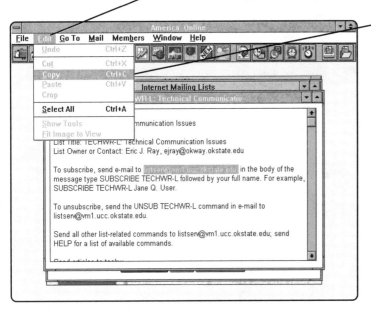

4. **Click** on the **Compose Mail icon** in the toolbar. The Compose Mail dialog box will appear.

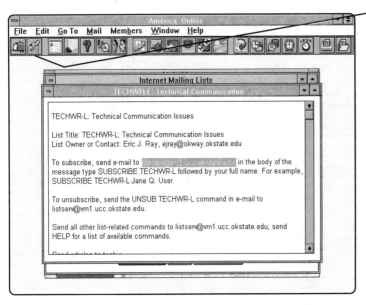

5. **Click** on **Edit** in the menu bar. A pull-down menu will appear.

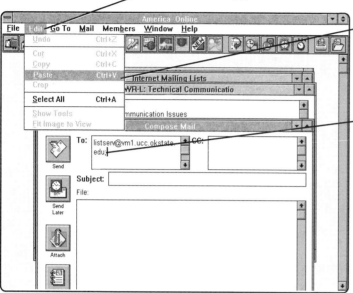

6. **Click** on **Paste**. The highlighted subscription address will appear in the To box.

7. If the highlighting carried over a semicolon at the end of the address, **press** the **Backspace key** to remove it.

8. **Press** the **Tab key** twice to move to the Subject box.

## Composing the Request

1. **Type** the **subject** of the message. **Press** the **Tab key** to move to the File box to type your message.

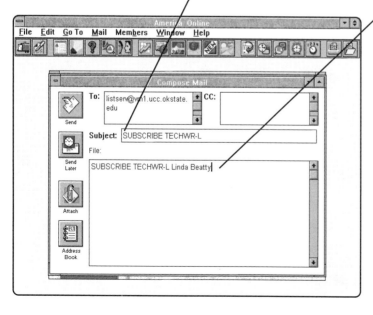

2. **Type** your **message**. This particular mailing list asks that you type "SUBSCRIBE TECHWR-L" followed by your real name in the body of the message. Some mailing-list subscriptions are handled by real people (what an astonishing concept), while others are processed by computer, as is this list (LISTSERV is a computer program). If the subscription directions tell you to send your request to a real person, please remember to put a "human touch" in your request.

## Sending the Request

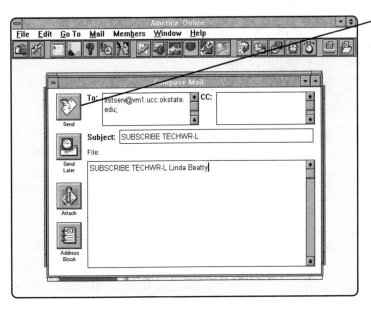

1. **Click** on the **Send button** in the Compose Mail dialog box.

2. When you see a message box saying that your mail has been sent, **click** on **OK** to close the message box.

Some lists take only minutes or hours to process your request. Almost all will be done by the next day. As soon as you are an official member of the mailing list, you'll start to receive mail.

## CLOSING ALL OPEN WINDOWS

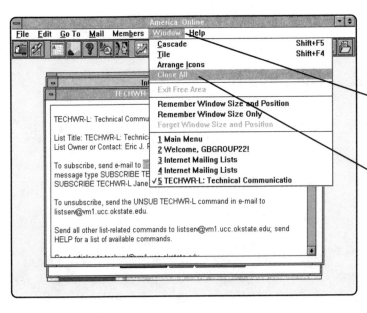

You can close all open windows with two clicks of your mouse.

1. **Click** on **Window** in the menu bar. A pull-down menu will appear.

2. **Click** on **Close All**. All open windows will be closed, and the opening Welcome screen will be minimized to an icon at the bottom of your screen.

## CONFIRMING YOUR REQUEST

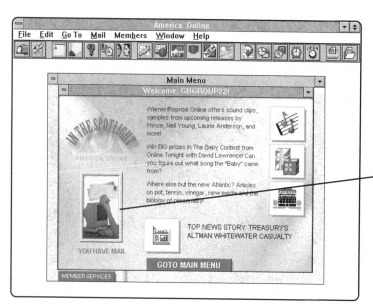

Some mailing lists require that you confirm your request. You'll get this message through the mail, often within hours. When you open AOL, you'll see that you have mail.

**1. Click twice** on the **You Have Mail icon**. The New Mail dialog box will appear.

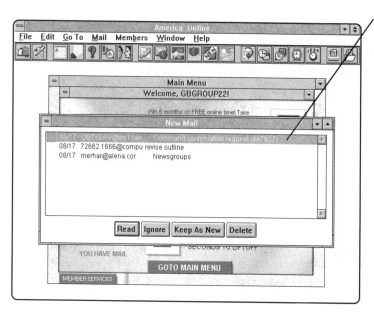

**2. Click twice** on the **Command confirmation request letter**. The letter will appear on your screen.

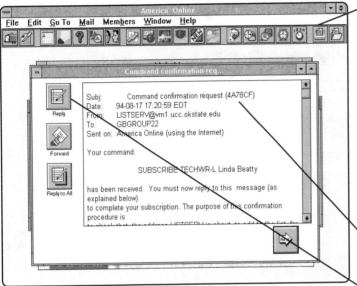

3. **Click** on the **Print icon** in the toolbar.

4. When the Print dialog box appears, **click** on **OK** to print the message.

5. **Read the message** carefully. It will contain specific directions for confirming your request.

Notice the Confirmation code in the Subject line.

6. **Click** on **Reply** to send your confirmation. The Reply dialog box will appear.

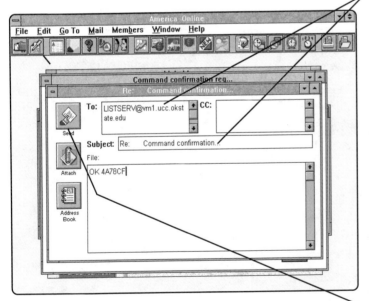

Notice that the address and the subject are already filled in.

7. **Click** in the File box to place the cursor.

8. **Type ok 4A78CF** (or whatever message the original letter from LISTSERV asked you to type). We found that it's best to include the confirmation code. Otherwise, you may have to resend your confirmation.

9. **Click** on **Send**. The message box saying that your mail has been sent will appear.

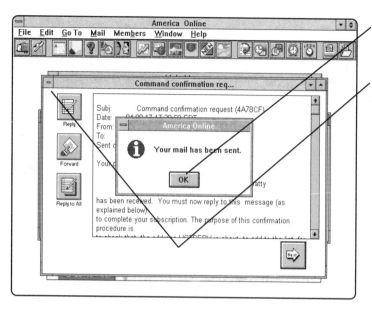

**10.** **Click** on **OK** to close the message box.

**11.** **Click twice** on the **Control menu box** (⊟) to close the mail window.

## CHECKING THE CONFIRMATION

You may receive a confirmation of your subscription within minutes or hours. It will be in your mailbox.

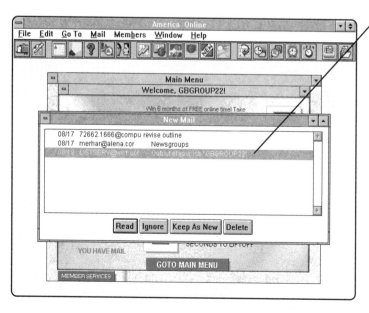

**1.** **Click twice** on the letter about the "**Output of your job.**" The letter will appear on your screen.

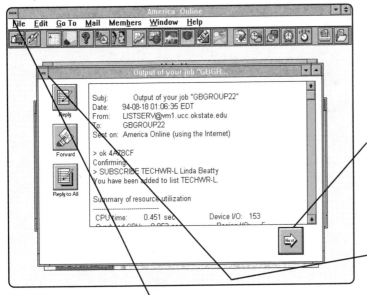

You are now an official member of this mailing list. You'll start receiving mail very shortly, sometimes within hours, and certainly by the next business day.

**2. Click** on the **Next arrow** to read your next piece of mail.

**OR**

**3. Click twice** on the **Control menu box** (⊟) to close the letter.

In Chapter 11, you'll learn how to contribute to a mailing list and how to resign, or unsubscribe, from a list. You can do all this off-line to save money.

**4.** If you're going on to Chapter 12, **click twice** on the **Control menu box** (⊟) on the right of the America Online title bar to close the program. When the dialog box appears, **click** on **Yes** to sign off and keep the AOL window on your screen.

# Contributing to and Resigning from an Internet Mailing List

When you first join an Internet mailing list, it's a good idea to spend time reading the correspondence before jumping right in. This way, you can learn the issues that are being discussed and get a sense of the protocols of the group. If you get lots of mail, we'll teach you a trick for managing it. If at any time you decide that the group is not for you, you can resign (unsubscribe). In this chapter, you will do the following:

❖ Add the mailing-list reply address to your Address Book
❖ Use a FlashSession to get your mail off-line
❖ Contribute to a mailing-list discussion
❖ Manage your mail
❖ Resign (unsubscribe) from a mailing list

## ADDING THE REPLY ADDRESS TO YOUR ADDRESS BOOK

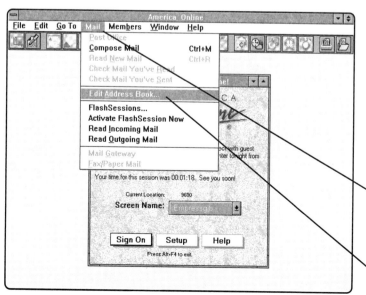

The description of the mailing list will give you a specific address for contributions. Add this address to your Address Book to make replying easy. You can edit your Address Book before you sign on to AOL.

1. **Click** on **Mail** in the menu bar. A pull-down menu will appear.

2. **Click** on **Edit Address Book**.

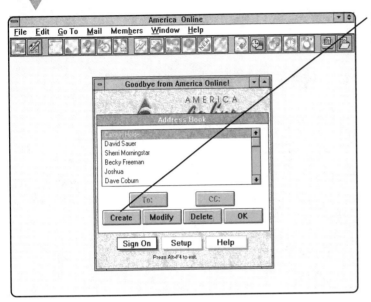

3. **Click** on **Create**. The Address Group dialog box will appear.

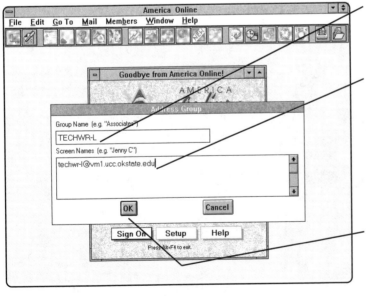

4. **Type** the **name** of the mailing list in the Group Name box.

5. **Type** the **address** in the Screen Names box. Internet names and addresses are not case-sensitive, so it doesn't matter whether you type the names in upper- or lowercase letters.

6. **Click** on **OK**. The Address Book dialog box will reappear.

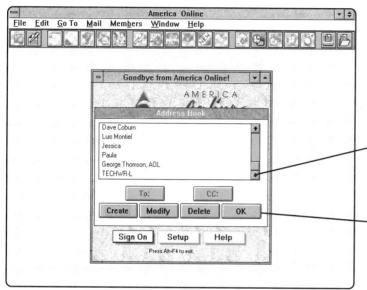

The new name has been added to the bottom of the Address Book list, so you may not see it until you scroll down to the bottom of the list.

7. **Click repeatedly** on ↓ to scroll to the bottom of the list to see the name.

8. **Click** on **OK** to add the name to your address book.

## SCHEDULING A FLASHSESSION FOR YOUR MAILING LIST MAIL

You can save money by reading your mail off-line. If you're not familiar with how FlashSessions work, see Chapter 8, "Using FlashSessions." In this next section, you'll switch to the screen name you created for mailing lists. If you didn't create a new screen name, skip steps 1 and 2 and go to step 3.

### Switching Screen Names

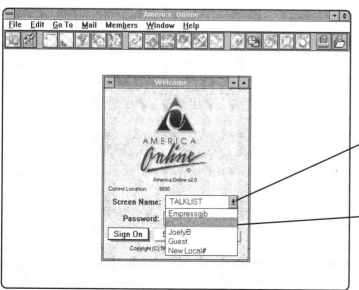

1. **Click** on ↓ to show a list of screen names you have created.

2. **Click** on the appropriate **screen name**. It will be placed in the Screen Name box.

3. **Click** on **Mail** in the menu bar. A pull-down menu will appear. If you did *not* create a separate screen name for your mailing list, go to step 4b.

4a. **Click** on **FlashSessions**. The FlashSessions dialog box will appear.

**OR**

4b. **Click** on **Activate FlashSession Now**, and then go to step 11.

5. **Click** on **Select Names**. The Select Screen Names dialog box will appear.

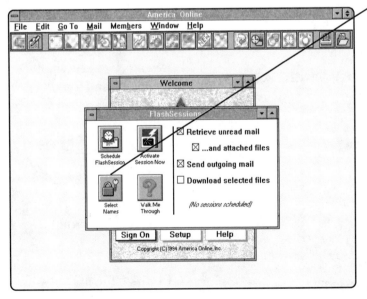

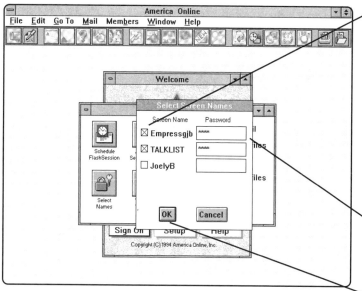

**6. Click** on the **name(s)** for which you want to run FlashSessions. If you don't want to run a FlashSession for a screen name that already has an ✕ beside it, click on the name to *remove* the ✕. This example shows that FlashSessions will be run for two screen names.

**7. Type** the **password** assigned to each screen name in the Password box.

**8. Click** on **OK**.

The directions on whether to retrieve unread mail and attached files, send mail, and download files are based on the selections you made when you set up your FlashSessions. You can change any option.

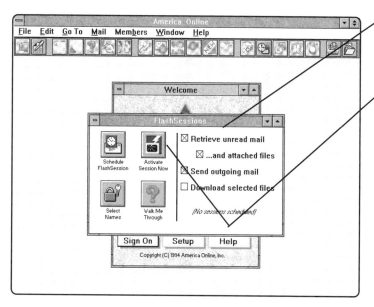

**9. Click** on the **appropriate option** to insert an ✕ in the box or to remove the ✕.

**10. Click** on **Activate Session Now** to start the session.

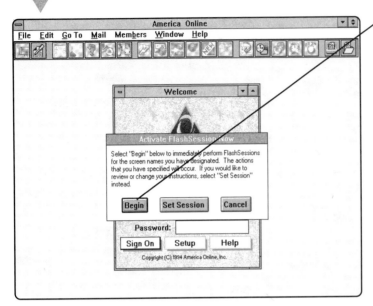

11. **Click** on **Begin**. AOL will sign itself on, download your mail, and then sign itself off. See Chapter 8, "Using FlashSessions," if you need help closing the FlashSession dialog box.

## READING MAILING-LIST CORRESPONDENCE

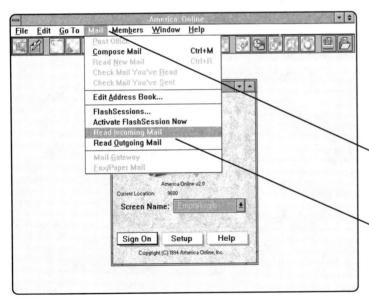

After you have downloaded your mail in a FlashSession, you can read it off-line. You can, of course, read your mail online, but it costs you online time and money.

1. **Click** on **Mail** in the menu bar. A pull-down menu will appear.

2. **Click** on **Read Incoming Mail**. The Incoming Flash Mail dialog box will appear with all your new mail.

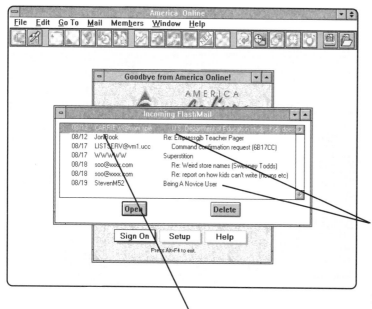

Each letter shows a date, the sender, and the subject. You can start reading at the top of the list or scroll through for an interesting-looking subject. Once you become familiar with the subject matter and contributors, you can look for specific names.

Mail sent from the mailing list appears indented in this dialog box. Mail sent directly to your screen name is not indented.

3. **Click twice** on the letter you want to read. It will appear on your screen. (You can also click once on the letter and then click on Open.)

Notice that the letter is addressed to you even though it came from the mailing list. This is because a mailing list sends a "copy" of each letter to every person on the list.

4. **Click** on **Next** to read the next letter on the list.

**OR**

**Click twice** on the **Control menu box** (☐) on the left of the letter's title bar to close the letter. You are then ready to select another letter to read.

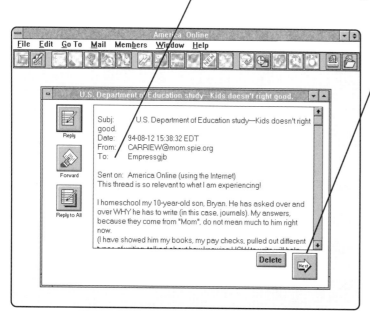

## UNDERSTANDING INTERNET ETIQUETTE

Before you begin contributing to a mailing list, you should be aware of Internet etiquette, or *netiquette,* as it is called.

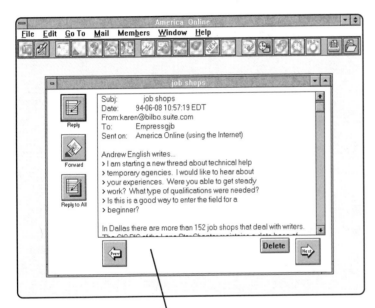

❖ Don't say anything in writing that you wouldn't say to someone's face with a roomful of people listening. Remember that Internet mail is read by millions of people.

❖ The reader doesn't have body language or tone of voice to help interpret your letter. For this reason, many people include such words as "smile," "shrug," and "wink" in parentheses after a sentence to help clarify intent.

❖ It can be helpful to refer to the original correspondence. If you quote someone, include her name. Copy the quoted text from the original letter and insert a > at the beginning of each line to show that it is a direct quote. You'll learn how to copy and paste between open windows later in this chapter.

This is an example of a response that quotes directly from a previous letter. Karen, the author of this letter, generously sent a detailed response to a request for information on "job shops." She included questions from the original request at the top of her response for readers who may not have seen the original letter.

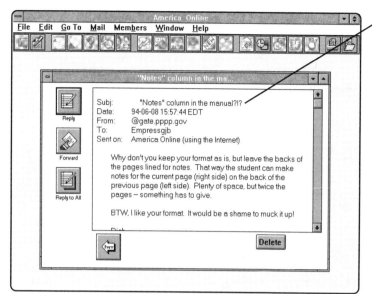

❖ You don't have to quote from a previous correspondence. Sometimes the subject line provides all the reference necessary, as in this helpful suggestion from Rich.

As you can see from these two examples, mailing lists can be a terrific source of professional advice. However, if you want to get help, be willing to give it.

## MAILING LIST PROTOCOL

In a mailing list, replies can be addressed to the individual who wrote the letter or, if the topic is of general interest, to the entire list. Each list has its own protocol for individual vs. group replies. If you spend a little time reading correspondence before jumping in, you'll be able to get a feel for how a particular list deals with this issue.

The examples in this section are based on the TechWr-L list. This list is set up so that replies go to the original author. If you want to send the reply to the list, you have to specifically enter the list address. The mailing list you join may be set up differently.

# CONTRIBUTING TO A MAILING LIST DISCUSSION

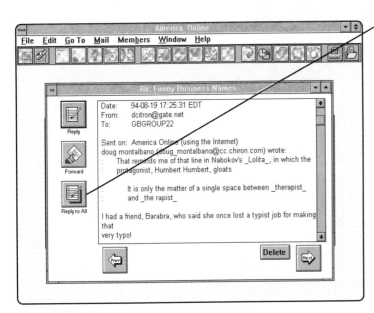

**1.** When the letter to which you want to reply is open, **click** on **Reply to All**. The Compose Mail dialog box will appear with the To and Subject boxes already filled in. Based on how your mailing list is set up, the reply will be addressed to the group or the individual.

## Changing the Address

In this example, the reply is set up by default to reply to the individual, so you'll have to use your Address Book to insert the list address into the To box. First, you'll erase the current address.

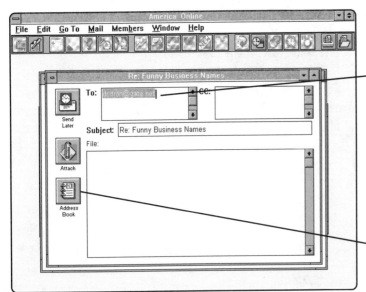

**1. Place** the **mouse pointer** at the end of the name and **click twice**. The name will be highlighted.

**2. Press** the **Delete** (Del) **key** to delete the highlighted text.

**3. Click** on **Address Book** to open the Address Book on your screen.

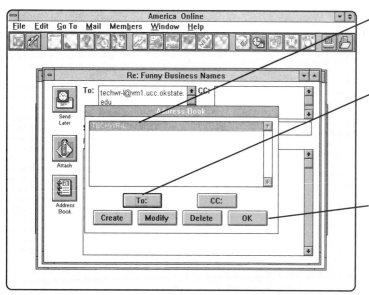

4. **Click** on the **address** of the mailing list to highlight it.

5. **Click** on **To** to insert the name into the To box of the letter. This example shows the address already inserted.

6. **Click** on **OK**.

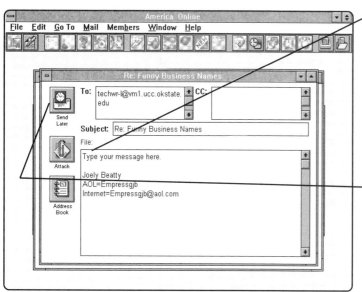

7. **Click inside** the message box and **type** your **message**. If you downloaded the Spell Check program described in Chapter 9, you can check your spelling and insert a signature line in one process.

8. **Click** on **Send Later**. You'll see a message saying your mail has been saved for later delivery. **Click** on **OK**.

If you decide that you don't want to send this letter, you can delete it from the list of Outgoing Mail. Simply click on Mail in the menu bar and then click on Check Outgoing Mail. A dialog box will appear that lists all mail that has been held for later delivery. Click on the letter, and then click on Delete.

# Copying and Pasting Between Open Windows

The example in this section shows a letter that has already been started. Now you decide that you want to quote some text from the original letter. It's easy to switch back and forth between open windows.

1. **Click** on **Window** in the menu bar. A pull-down menu will appear. A list of all open windows will be at the bottom of the menu.

2. **Click** on the **name** of the original letter. In this example, it is "It's a Journalism thing...." You will be returned to that letter.

3. **Place** the mouse arrow to the **left** of the text you want to copy. (You can't click to place the cursor as you would normally do in a Windows program.) **Press and hold** the **mouse button** and **drag** the mouse **over** the **text**. It will be highlighted.

4. **Click** on **Edit** in the menu bar.

5. **Click** on **Copy**. You won't see any difference in your screen, but the highlighted text will be copied to the Clipboard.

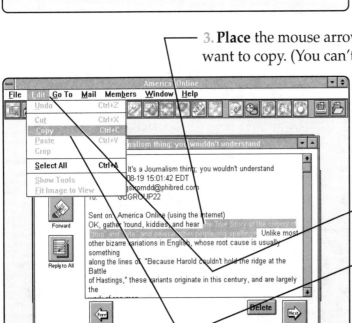

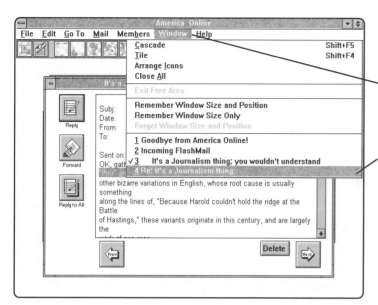

Now you have to go back to your response.

**6.** **Click** on **Window** in the menu bar. A pull-down menu will appear.

**7.** **Click** on your **reply** letter. In this example, it is "Re: It's a Journalism thing;" You will be returned to your reply letter.

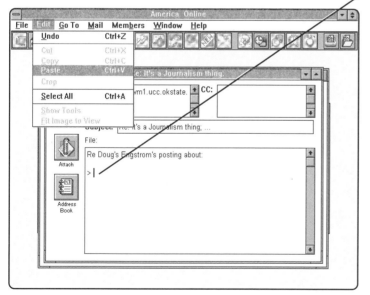

**8.** **Click** in the **letter** where you want to place the text and **type** a > and **press** the **spacebar**.

**9.** **Click** on **Edit** in the menu bar. A pull-down menu will appear.

**10.** **Click** on **Paste**. The text from the original letter will appear in your reply letter.

**11.** **Type** your **message**, and then **click** on **Send Later**.

## INTRODUCING A NEW TOPIC

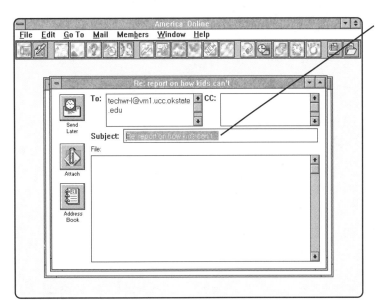

You introduce a new topic, or *thread*, by typing a new subject in the Subject box.

1. **Open** a **letter** (it doesn't matter what the letter is). **Click** on **Reply to All** when a letter is on your screen.

2. **Place** the **mouse arrow** in the **Subject box** at the start of the text. **Press and hold** the **mouse button** and **drag** the highlight bar **over** the existing **text**.

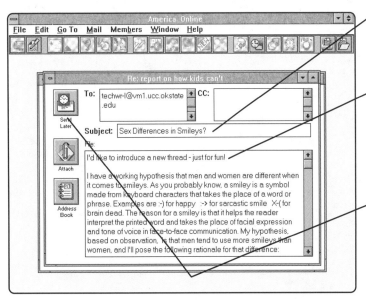

3. **Type** the **new topic**. It will replace the highlighted text.

4. **Type** your **message** in the File box. Complete your spell-check if you have an appropriate program to do so.

5. **Click** on **Send Later**. **Click** on **OK** when the message box appears, telling you that your mail has been sent.

## SAVING MAIL

Even though you're off-line, you can save individual letters.

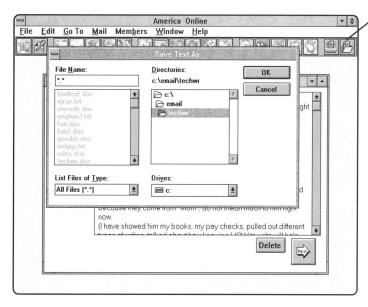

1. When the letter you want is on your screen, **click** on the **Save icon** in the toolbar. The Save As dialog box will appear.

2. **Repeat** steps 2 through 7 on page 64 to save a letter.

## DELETING MAIL

When you download mail, it is copied to your hard drive, where it can take up quite a lot of space.

1. **Click** on the **letter** you want to delete to highlight it.

2. **Click** on **Delete**. You'll see message boxes asking if you want to delete the letter. **Click** on **Yes**.

You can delete each letter individually, but if you get a lot of mail, that process can result in a severe case of carpal tunnel syndrome from repeated mouse clickings. If you created a separate screen name for your mailing list, check out the next section for a real timesaving tip!

# DELETING DOWNLOADED MAIL FROM YOUR HARD DRIVE

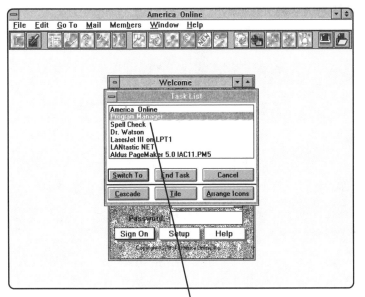

Once you've saved the letters you really want, you can get rid of all the downloaded mail with one time-saving device.

## Switching to File Manager

To do this next procedure, you need to switch to File Manager.

**1. Press and hold** the **Ctrl key** and **press** the **Esc key** (Ctrl + Esc). The Task List dialog box will appear on your screen.

**2. Click twice** on **Program Manager** to switch to that window.

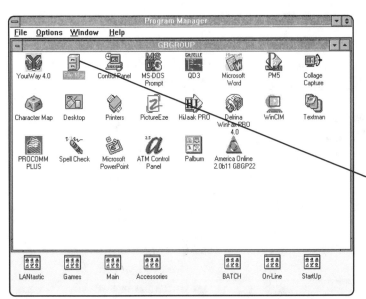

**3. Open** the **group** that contains File Manager. We moved our File Manager to a customized group window. Your File Manager icon may be in the Main group window.

**4. Click twice** on the **File Manager icon**. The File Manager window will open on your screen.

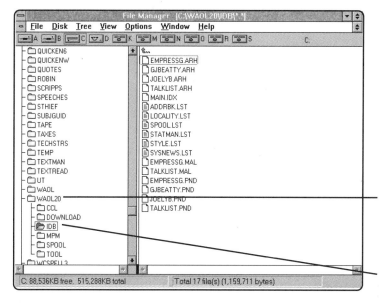

## Finding the Download Directories

AOL downloads mail to the IDB directory, which AOL created when you installed it.

1. **Click twice** on **WAOL20** to show all the sub-directories.

2. **Click** on **IDB** to show a list of files in this directory.

3. **Click** on **View** in the menu bar. A pull-down menu will appear.

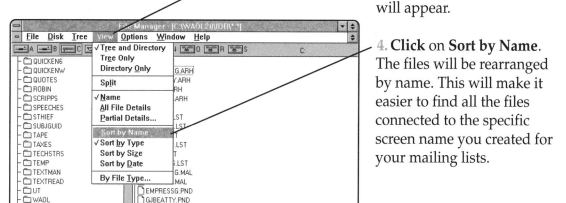

4. **Click** on **Sort by Name**. The files will be rearranged by name. This will make it easier to find all the files connected to the specific screen name you created for your mailing lists.

## Deleting Downloaded Mail

All of the downloaded mail is contained in three files in the IDB directory. The files have your screen name and the extensions ARH, MAL, and PND. You have to delete all three files to clear up the mail. If you've run a FlashSession for more than one screen name, each screen name will have these three files. In this section, we'll delete the files for the screen name TALKLIST.

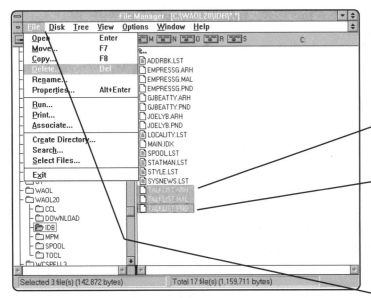

1. **Click** on **TALKLIST.ARH** to highlight it.

2. **Press and hold** the **Shift key** and **click** on **TALKLIST.PND**. All files between clicks will be highlighted.

3. When the files are highlighted, **click** on **File** in the menu bar, and then **click** on **Delete**. The Delete dialog box will appear on your screen, showing the names of the files you want to delete.

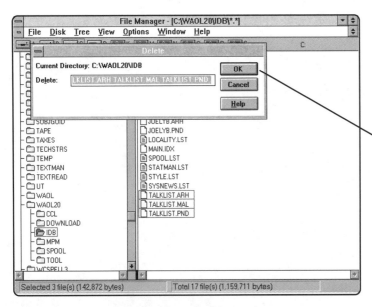

4. **Click** on **OK**. You'll see a Confirm File Delete dialog box.

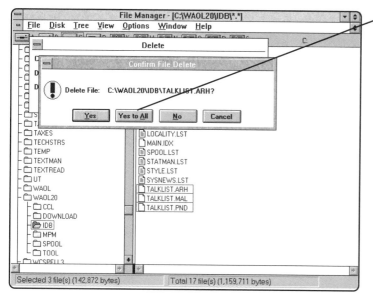

5. **Click** on **Yes to All** to delete all three files. Any mail for this screen name that was not previously saved is now deleted.

Isn't this a quick and easy way to clean up your mail?

## RESIGNING FROM A MAILING LIST

You can at any time resign, or *unsubscribe*, from a mailing list. If you didn't keep a copy of the mailing-list description, it's easy enough to get. It contains the exact directions for unsubscribing.

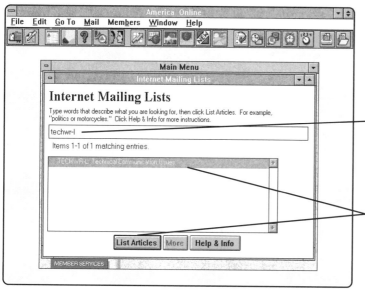

1. **Repeat steps 1 through 4** in the section "Searching for a Mailing List" on page 127 to open the Internet Mailing Lists dialog box.

2. **Type** the **name** of the mailing list from which you want **to resign**. In this example, it is techwr-l.

3. **Click** on **List Articles** to see the listing, and then **click twice** on the **listing** to open it up for printing.

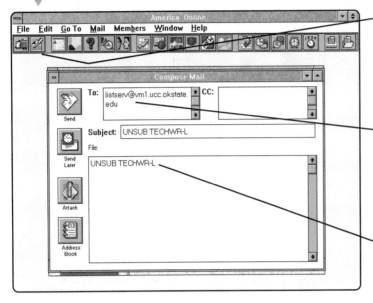

**4.** When you have printed the directions, **click** on the **Compose Mail icon** in the toolbar. It's the second icon from the left.

**5. Type** the **correct address** in the To box. This address is always different from the one you used to send mail to the list.

**6. Type** the appropriate **message** in the Compose Mail dialog box. It is usually UNSUB plus the name of the mailing list.

**7. Click** on **Send Later** if you're off-line, or Send if you're online.

## Thanks

The examples in this chapter are real and come from members of the TechWr-L mailing list. The professional generosity among list members and their tremendous good sense and humor are examples of what makes the Internet vital and exciting.

We'd like to thank the list owner, Eric J. Ray, who took the time to answer numerous questions. List members Michele Berkes, John P. Brinegar, David H. Citron, Andrew English, Douglas Engstrom, Margaret Gerard, Douglas Montalbano, Richard G. Sobocinski, and Karen Steele gave us permission to use their correspondence as examples and/or gave us valuable advice. Thanks.

# Reading Newsgroups

Newsgroups are not "news." They can best be described as "worldwide discussion groups," in which people post and read messages on many different topics. Newsgroups are among the most interesting and popular options on the Internet. Newsgroups are sometimes referred to in Internet talk as USENET news, Net news, Internet news, news, and, of course, newsgroups. As of this writing, there are over 11,000 newsgroups, many of which are available through AOL. The list of newsgroups is updated on an almost daily basis. It's a good idea to read a newsgroup's messages to get a feel for that particular newsgroup's culture before you actually contribute or respond to a discussion. In this chapter, you will do the following:

❖ Read a newsgroup message and then print and save it
❖ Close a newsgroup
❖ Mark a newsgroup as having been read

## READING NEWSGROUPS

America Online makes it easy to read messages in a newsgroup. However, as you will discover, one of the problems is that there are so many messages! In this section, you will read a message from a list of topics in a newsgroup.

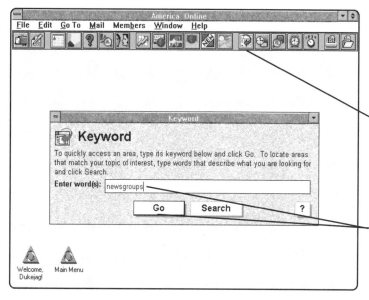

1. **Click** on the **Keyword icon** in the toolbar. It's the seventh from the right. The Keyword dialog box will appear.

2. **Type newsgroups** and **click** on **Go**. The Newsgroups dialog box will appear.

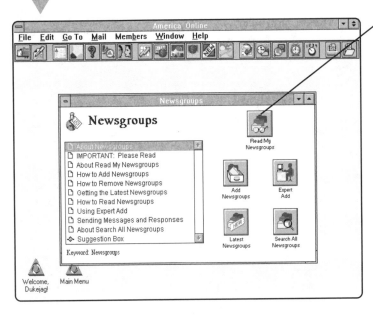

3. **Click** on the **Read My Newsgroups button**. The Read My Newsgroups dialog box will appear. You may get a "message of the day" dialog box first. If so, click on OK.

**Note:** The newsgroups located in the Read My Newsgroups dialog box were selected by AOL's staff to help you get started in contributing to newsgroups. You can change your Read My Newsgroups dialog box to contain newsgroups geared toward your interests by adding or removing newsgroups. See Chapter 13, "Adding, Contributing To, and Removing Newsgroups."

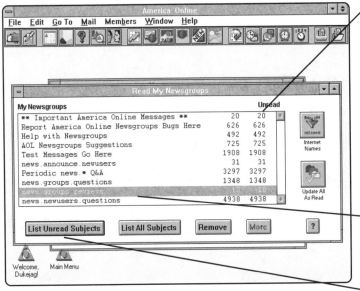

Notice that the Unread column tells you how many messages you have not read in the newsgroup. Seeing a newsgroup with over 4,000 unread messages can seem a bit overwhelming at first, but AOL helps you narrow down the options, as you will see later in this chapter.

4. **Click** on the **newsgroup** you want to explore to highlight it.

5. **Click** on **List Unread Subjects**. A dialog box containing the unread messages in this newsgroup will appear.

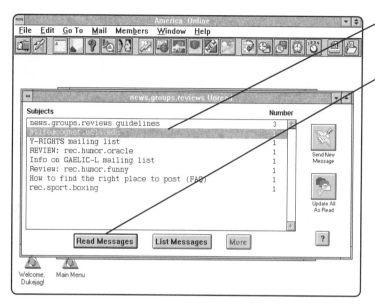

**6. Click** on the **topic** of your choice to highlight it.

**7. Click** on **Read Messages**. The first message on the topic you chose will appear in a dialog box. The subject of the message will appear in the title bar of the dialog box.

 **Note:** Although in this example there is only one message to read, it is important to understand that some discussion topics within a newsgroup will have *numerous* messages attached to them. This is because more than one person has sent feedback to the discussion.

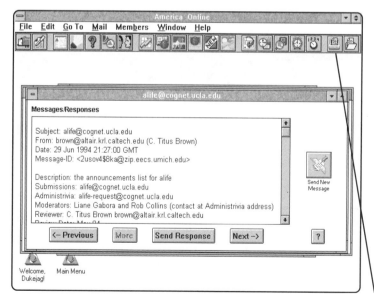

## PRINTING THE MESSAGE

You can read the message online by clicking on the ⬇ on the scroll bar or you can print it and read it later offline. Obviously, your meter is running when you read online, so we recommend that you print (or save) the message for later, more in-depth reading.

**1. Click** on the **Print icon** in the toolbar. It's the second icon from the right. The Print Text dialog box will appear.

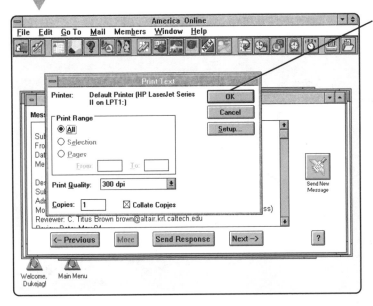

2. Click on OK. The message will print and the dialog box will disappear.

## SAVING THE MESSAGE

If you want to keep an electronic copy of the file for later use, you can save the file. The file will be saved in a text-file format, but you can give it any name and extension you want. In this section, we gave the file a ".doc" extension so that we could open it easily in Word for Windows.

1. Click on the Save icon in the toolbar. It's the first one on the right. The Save As dialog box as shown here will appear.

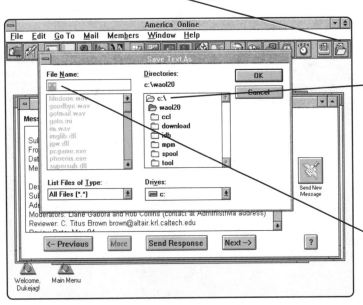

2. Click twice on c:\ to show a list of all directories on the C drive.

3. Click twice on the directory where you want to save the message.

4. Type a filename and an extension.

5. Click on OK if you want to save this message. The dialog box will disappear and the file will be saved.

# CLOSING A NEWSGROUP

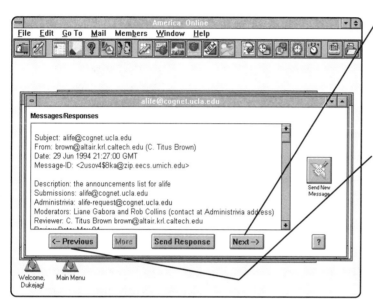

1. If you want to read additional messages on this topic, **click** on **Next** in the lower right corner of the dialog box to read the next message.

2. **Click** on the **Previous button** as many times as necessary to return to the previous messages.

3. **Click twice** on the **Control menu box** (⊟) on the left of the title bar. The dialog box will close.

4. **Click twice** on the **Control menu box** (⊟) on the left of the Subject dialog box title bar. The dialog box will close.

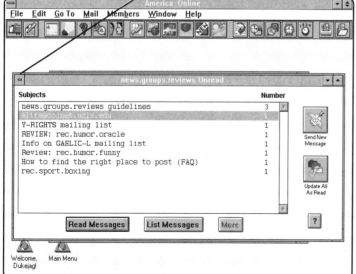

# MARKING NEWSGROUPS
# AS HAVING BEEN READ

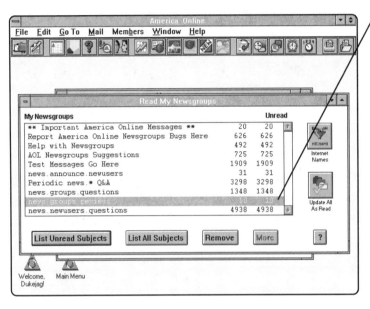

The Internet is chock-full of useful and not-so-useful information. Newsgroups are no exception. Can you imagine trying to read over 4,000 messages in this newsgroup? Fortunately, you can read selected messages in a newsgroup and then mark the entire newsgroup as having been read. When you do this, the next time you go to that newsgroup, only the new, unread messages will be on your reading list. That's the good news. The bad news is that you cannot mark selected *topics* in a newsgroup as unread. It's either all or none.

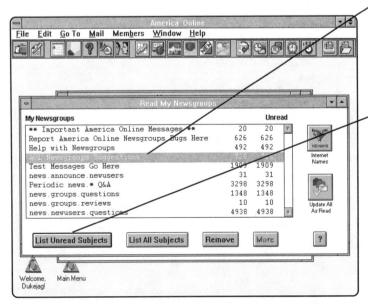

1. **Click** on the **newsgroup** you want to mark to highlight it. In this example, we used AOL Newsgroups Suggestions.

2. **Click** on **List Unread Subjects**. A Subjects dialog box will appear.

**3. Click** on **Update All As Read button**. An untitled dialog box will appear in the foreground.

**WARNING:** If you click on OK in step 4 below, *all the messages in the entire newsgroup at this time will no longer be available for you to read.* Only those messages that arrive after you have marked this newsgroup will be available for you to read.

**4. Click** on **Cancel** if you don't want to delete all the messages.

**5.** If you are absolutely certain that you do not want to return to these messages for further reading, **click** on **OK**. Nothing will happen right now. However, when you close the Read My Newsgroups dialog box and then reopen it, the number of messages available for reading in the AOL Newsgroups Suggestions will be "0." A zero will appear in the left column.

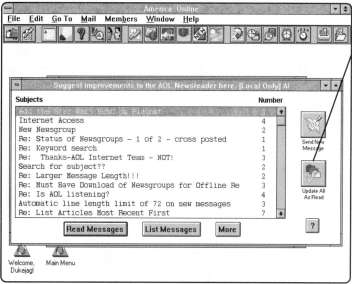

# Adding, Contributing to, and Removing Newsgroups

As of this writing, there are over 11,000 newsgroups available through America Online. The newsgroups in your Read My Newsgroups section are just samples that the AOL people put there for you to review. You can add newsgroups by using the Add Newsgroups option, the Latest Newsgroups option, or the Expert Add option. You can also contribute to a newsgroup and remove a newsgroup. In this chapter, you will do the following:

❖ Add a newsgroup to your Read My Newsgroup list
❖ Contribute to a newsgroup
❖ Add another newsgroup using Search All Newsgroups
❖ Add additional newsgroups using Latest Newsgroups and Expert Add
❖ Remove a newsgroup

## ADDING A NEWSGROUP

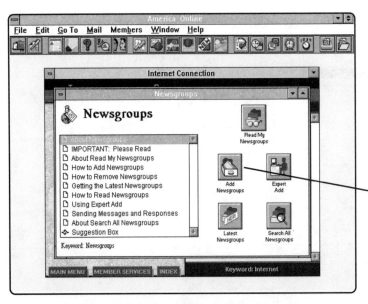

In this section, you will select a newsgroup and add it to the Read My Newsgroups list.

1. **Connect** to **AOL** and **open Newsgroups** if you have not already done so.

2. **Click** on the **Add Newsgroups icon**. The Add Newsgroups Categories dialog box will appear.

**3. Click** on **a category** that strikes your fancy. In this example, we clicked on Business and Commercial Newsgroups.

**Note:** If you want to see the rest of the list, you can click on More and then click repeatedly on the ⬇ to scroll down the list.

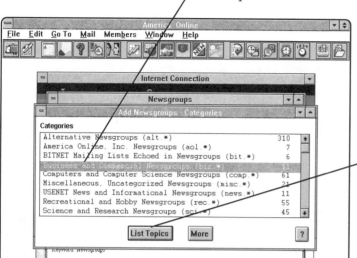

**4. Click** on **List Topics**. The Business and Commercial Newsgroups Topics dialog box will appear.

**5. Click** on **a topic** that looks interesting. In this example, we clicked on Computer Business Groups.

**6. Click** on **List Newsgroups**. The Computer Business Groups Newsgroups dialog box will appear.

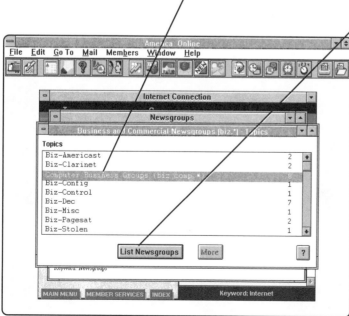

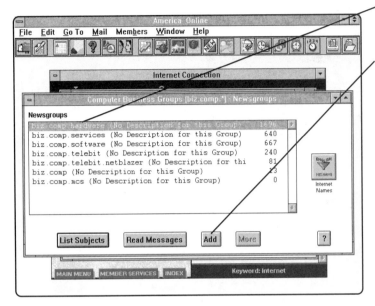

7. **Click** on **biz.comp.hardware**.

8. **Click** on **Add**. An untitled dialog box will appear.

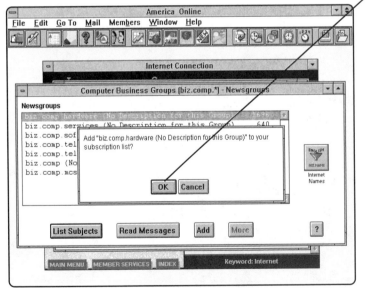

9. **Click** on **OK**. The untitled dialog box will disappear and an America Online dialog box will appear.

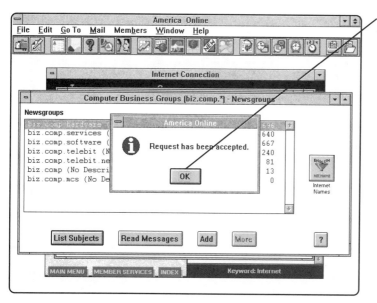

**10. Click** on **OK**. The dialog box will disappear.

## Closing Add Newsgroups

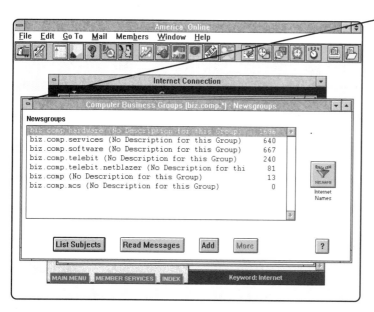

**1. Click twice** on the ⊟ of all the open dialog boxes to return to the Newsgroups dialog box you see in the next example.

# Viewing Your Newly Added Newsgroup

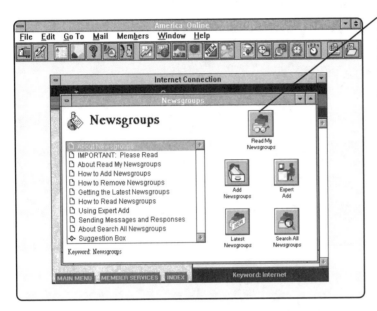

1. **Click** on **Read My Newsgroups**. The Read My Newsgroups dialog box will appear. (You may get a newsgroup-of-the-day dialog box. If you do, click on OK.)

2. **Click** on your **newly added newsgroup**. In this example, it is the biz.comp.hardware newsgroup.

3. **Click** on **List All Subjects**. The Biz-Comp-Hardware dialog box will appear.

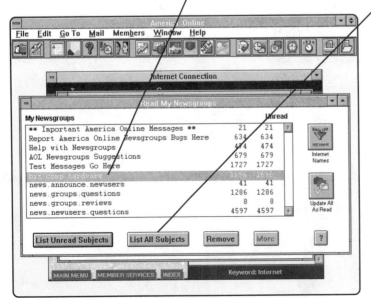

# CONTRIBUTING TO A NEWSGROUP

Before contributing to a newsgroup, please review the etiquette suggestions in Chapter 11, the section entitled "Understanding Internet Etiquette." You can add to your credibility as a newsgroup contributor by adding your name, organization, and other identifying information to your closing. You do not have to do this, but it does tell the readers that you are a serious contributor.

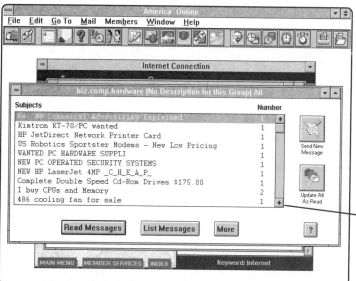

1. **Click repeatedly** on the ↓ to scroll down the list of subjects in this newsgroup.

2. **Click twice** on a **subject** that interests you. In this example, we clicked on MOSAIC NEEDED.

Notice that only two messages are shown on this subject. If there were many messages, click on List Messages. A list of all the messages will appear in a dialog box. From this list, you can select the messages you want to read.

3. **Click** on **Read Messages**. A MOSAIC NEEDED dialog box will appear.

## Sending A Response

In this example, you will send a response to the person who originated the subject. If there are responses already listed under the subject, it's a good idea to read them first before responding, to avoid duplication.

1. **Click** on **Send Response**. A dialog box will appear. The Send To and Subject boxes will be filled in. Also, a sentence showing the message to which you are replying and the author's address will be filled in at the top of the text box.

2. **Type** your **response** in the Response text box. To follow "Netiquette," make sure that you "quote" from the request above, as we have here. See Chapter 11, the section entitled "Understanding Internet Etiquette" for tips on quoting.

Notice that we inserted a closing containing our AOL and Internet addresses.

3. **Click** on **Send**. An AOL dialog box will appear.

**4. Click** on **OK**. The dialog box will disappear.

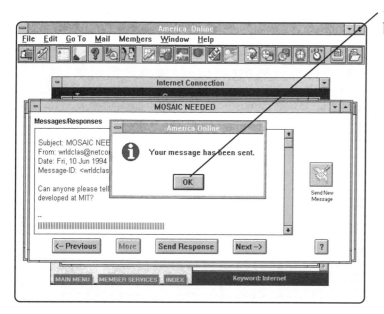

## Creating Your Own Message

The message you just sent will be added to the list of responses to a subject created by someone else. In this section, you will create your own "subject" to which other people can respond.

**1. Click** on the **Send New Message icon**. A Post New Message dialog box will appear.

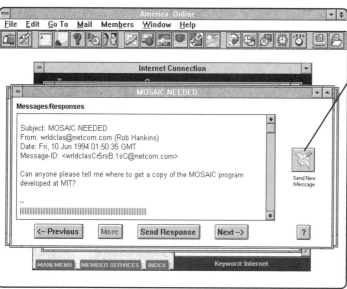

**2. Type** a **subject heading**. If you want to get attention, sometimes it helps to type in all caps. This worked because four people responded in the same day!

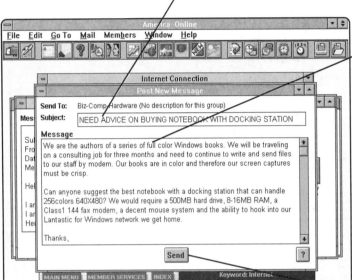

**3. Type** your **message** in the Message text box. If you want serious replies, make sure that you include your name, address, organization, etc. Because we followed Netiquette guidelines, we received four e-mail replies. In each case, it was obvious that the respondents took the time to give us good information.

**4. Click** on **Send**. An America Online dialog box will appear.

**5. Click** on **OK**. The dialog box will disappear.

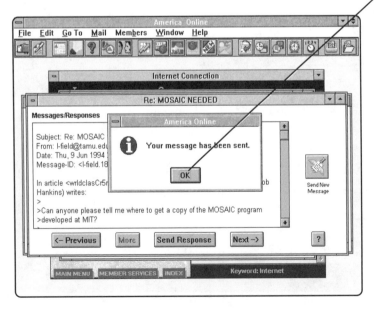

# ADDING MORE NEWSGROUPS

In addition to adding newsgroups to your Read My Newsgroups list with the Add Newsgroup icon, there are three other ways you can add newsgroups to your personal reading list. In this section, you will add a newsgroup with each of these methods: (1) the Latest Newsgroups icon, (2) the Search All Newsgroups icon, and (3) the Expert Add icon.

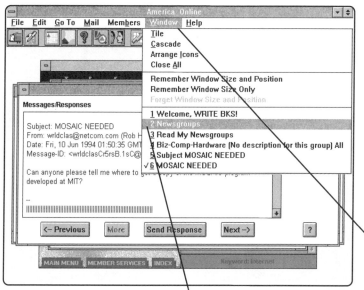

## Using Latest Newsgroups

1. **Click** on **Window** in the menu bar. A pull-down menu will appear.

2. **Click** on **Newsgroups**. The Newsgroups dialog box will appear.

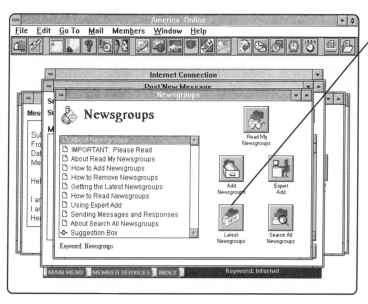

3. **Click** on the **Latest Newsgroups icon**. The Latest Newsgroups dialog box will appear.

**Note:** You may get a message that says "No newsgroups have been added since your last visit." In that case, click on OK on the message box.

**4. Click** on a **newsgroup** you want to add to your list. In this example, we were intrigued by "Renaissance Faires."

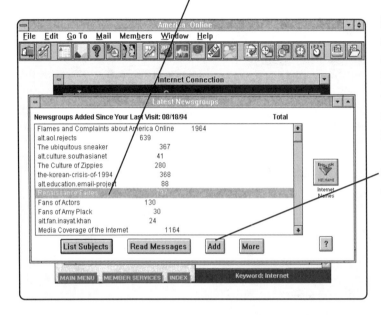

**5.** If a newsgroup's title doesn't tell you enough, **click** on the **List Subjects button** to read more about the group. Then close the dialog box and go to the next step.

**6. Click** on **Add**. An untitled dialog box will appear.

**7. Click** on **OK**. The untitled dialog box will disappear. An America Online dialog box will appear.

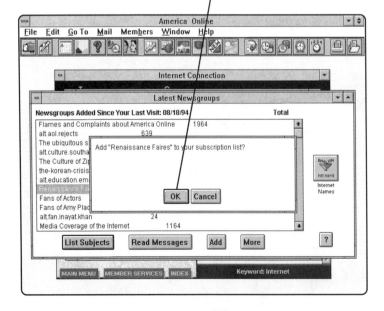

8. **Click** on **OK**. The dialog box will disappear.

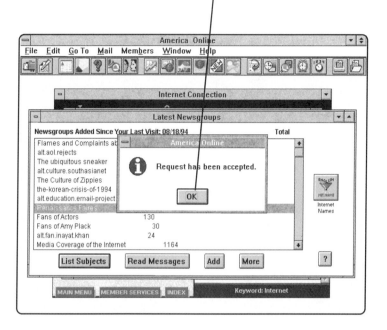

## Using Search All Newsgroups

1. **Click twice** on ⊟ in the left corner of the Latest Newsgroups title bar. The Latest Newsgroups dialog box will close.

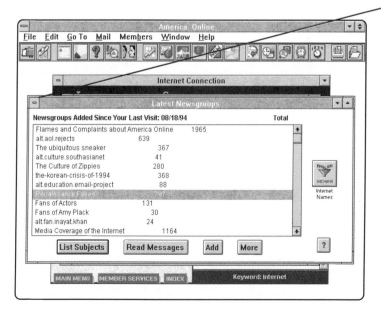

**2. Click** on the **Search All Newsgroups icon**. The Search All Newsgroups dialog box will appear.

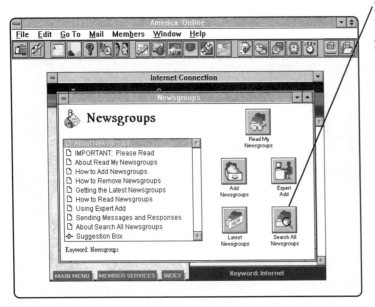

**3. Type** a **topic name**. In this example, we were interested in finding movie reviews.

**4. Click** on the **Search button**. The Search Results dialog box will appear with a list of newsgroups on the topic.

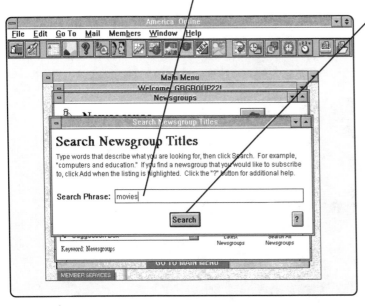

5. **Click** on the **name** of the **newsgroup** you want to select.

6. **Click** on the **View De- scription button**. A News- group Description dialog box will appear.

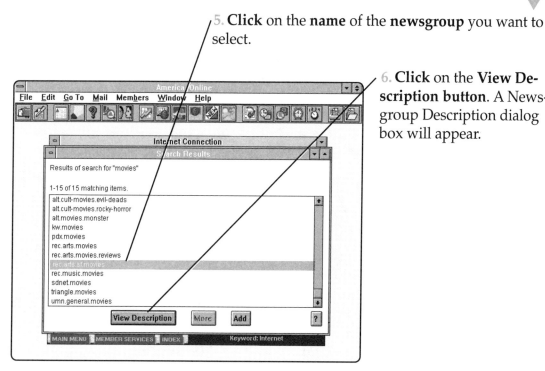

7. **Click** on **OK**. The dialog box will disappear.

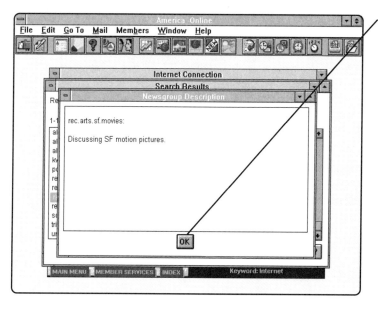

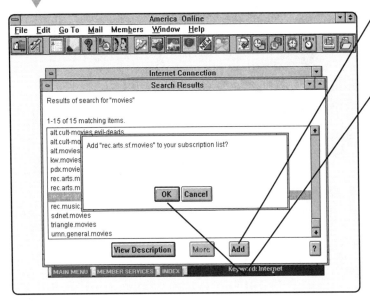

**8. Click** on **Add**. An untitled dialog box will appear (shown here).

**9. Click** on **OK**. The untitled dialog box will disappear, and an America Online dialog box will appear. **Click** on **OK**.

## Using Expert Add

If you know the Internet name of a newsgroup and simply want to add it to your list, then the Expert Add icon is the ticket! You can find the names of hundreds of newsgroups in the Internet reference books available in public libraries or in bookstores.

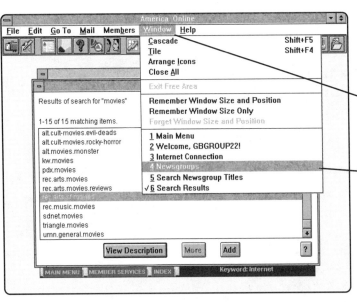

**1. Click** on **Window** in the menu bar. A pull-down menu will appear.

**2. Click** on **Newsgroups**. The Newsgroups dialog box will appear.

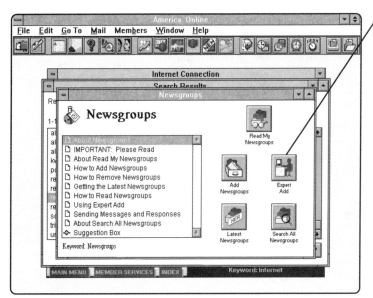

3. **Click** on the **Expert Add icon**. The Expert Add dialog box will appear.

4. **Type** the **Internet name** of the newsgroup you want to add to your list.

5. **Click** on **Add**. An untitled dialog box will appear.

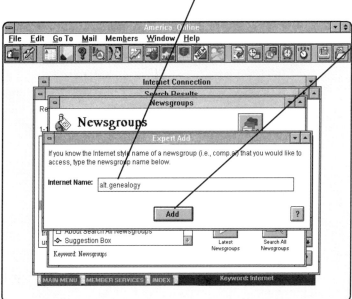

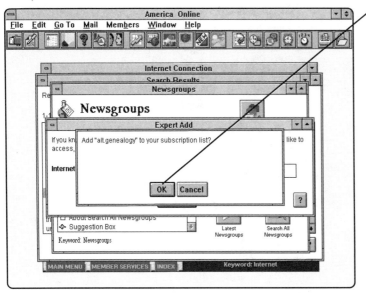

6. **Click** on **OK**. An America Online dialog box will appear, saying that your request has been accepted. **Click** on **OK**.

## REMOVING A NEWSGROUP

Newsgroups are not always what they appear to be in their descriptions. Some are great. Some are not so great. In fact, you may have added a newsgroup to your list that, from your point of view, contains a lot of useless information. Fortunately, you can remove it from your newsgroup reading list with the click of a mouse.

1. **Click** on **Window** in the menu bar. A pull-down menu will appear.

2. **Click** on **Newsgroups**. The Newsgroups dialog box will appear.

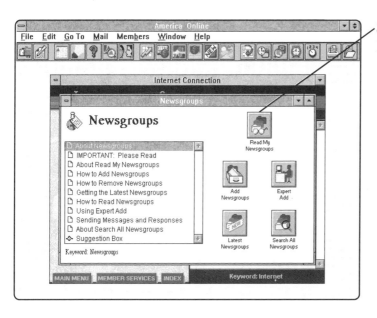

3. **Click** on the **Read My Newsgroups icon**.

4. **Click** on the **name** of the **newsgroup** *you want to remove*.

5. **Click** on **Remove**. An untitled dialog box will appear (shown here).

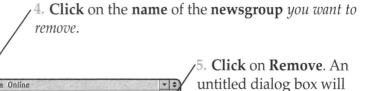

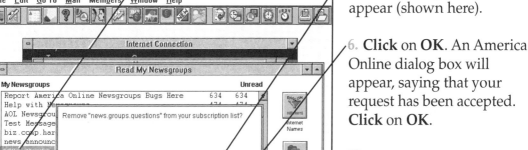

6. **Click** on **OK**. An America Online dialog box will appear, saying that your request has been accepted. **Click** on **OK**.

The newsgroup you removed will remain on your list until you close Read My Newsgroups. When you reopen the Read My Newsgroups dialog box, it will no longer be on your reading list.

# Cruising the Internet Using Gopher

Gopher is the name of computer programs that make using the Internet easier by giving you a menu of items to choose from. These items can be text files that you can read and save or connections to other gophers at other computers. It's called "gopher" after the mascot of the University of Minnesota, where the original program was developed, and because it does the "underground" work of moving you around the Internet. America Online's gopher lets you go from computer to computer as though you were out for a Sunday drive. In this chapter, you will do the following:

❖ Use the AOL gopher to do some random Internet touring
❖ Set up AOL to automatically scroll documents as they are received

## OPENING GOPHER

1. **Sign on to America Online** if you haven't already done so and **click** on the ▼s of both the Welcome screen and Main Menu to minimize them.

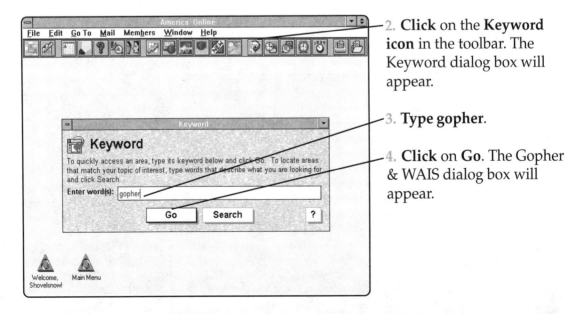

2. **Click** on the **Keyword icon** in the toolbar. The Keyword dialog box will appear.

3. **Type gopher**.

4. **Click** on **Go**. The Gopher & WAIS dialog box will appear.

## CHECKING THE LIST OF TOPICS

The Main Categories listed here were selected by the AOL gopher team as starting points for exploring the Internet.

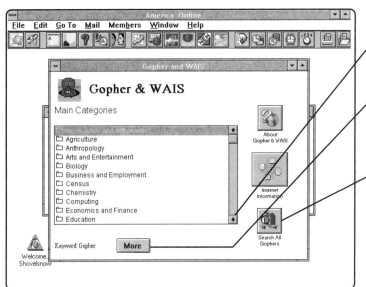

1. **Click repeatedly** on the ⬇ to scroll down the list.

2. **Click** on **More** to view the rest of the list.

❖ The Search All Gophers button starts the "Veronica" program. We'll explain Veronica's special features in Chapter 15.

## HEADING DOWN THE INTERNET HIGHWAY

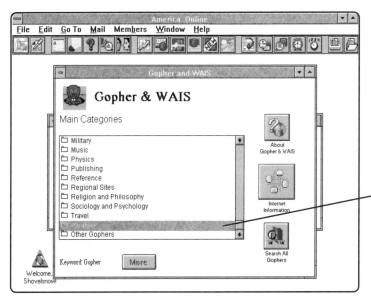

Internet cruising is like taking a pleasure drive, turning left or right at random to go down roads you've never seen. Let's explore the weather highway first.

1. **Click twice** on **Weather**. The Weather dialog box will appear.

**2. Click twice** on **WAIS weather server**. The WAIS weather server dialog box will appear.

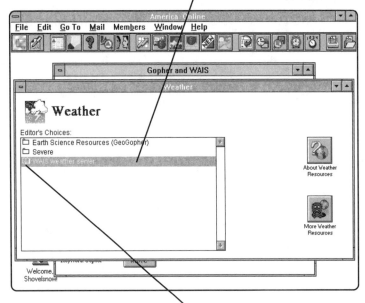

❖ WAIS (pronounced "ways") stands for Wide Area Information Server. WAIS is another program, like gopher, that is used to search on the Internet. A WAIS is set up to search for words that occur in files contained in computer databases.

❖ An open-book icon in AOL's gopher menus means that a WAIS program is there to help you search for information in the computer(s) to which gopher has connected you. WAIS searches by "keyword." You tell the WAIS what word or words to search for, and it lists the files that contain the word(s). (See the section "Reviewing Keyword Search" in Chapter 15.)

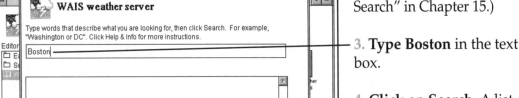

**3. Type Boston** in the text box.

**4. Click** on **Search**. A list of documents that contain the word "Boston" will appear.

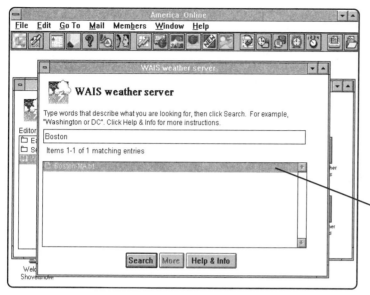

The WAIS weather server found only one item. If we had used New York or San Diego, it would have found more (the WAIS would list several cities' names starting with "New" and "San").

5. **Click twice** on **Boston-MA.txt**. The Boston weather report and forecast will appear in a dialog box called Boston-MA.txt.

## Scrolling Versus More

When your computer receives a long file, you can see only a portion of the file on your screen at first. When you have scrolled down to the bottom of the file and the More button remains active, clicking on More brings up more of the file.

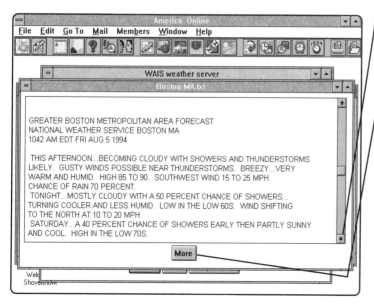

1. **Click repeatedly** on the ⬇ to scroll down the file so that you can read what's happening. What a surprise! Rain in Boston!

2. **Click** on **More** to see the rest of the report. *If More is grayed out, it means that you are at the end of the file.* You can set up AOL to automatically scroll to the end of the file. See the section "Setting the Automatic Scrolling Option," later in this chapter.

## SAVING A FILE

You can save this weather report as a text file. If there's a More button at the bottom of its dialog box, click on it and scroll down to be sure that you have the whole file.

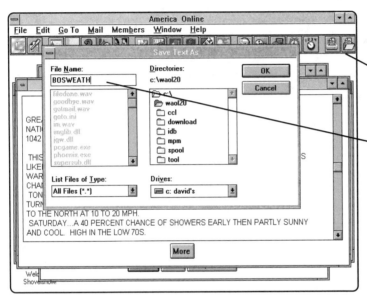

**1. Click** on the **Save icon** the toolbar. The Save As dialog box will appear.

**2. Type a name.**

**3. Click** on **OK.** The file will be copied to the directory on your computer shown in the Save As window (or you can type a path to a specific directory and then click on OK.)

## PRINTING A FILE

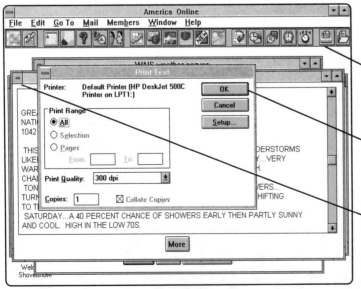

Printing is just as easy.

**1. Click** the **Print icon** in the toolbar. The Print dialog box will open.

**2. Click** on **OK.** The Print dialog box will close and the file will print.

**3. Click twice** on the ⊟ in the left corner of the Boston-MA.txt title bar. The dialog box will close.

## GOING BACK TO A FAMILIAR INTERSECTION

If you start getting lost on your Internet roadtrip, you might want to return to familiar territory.

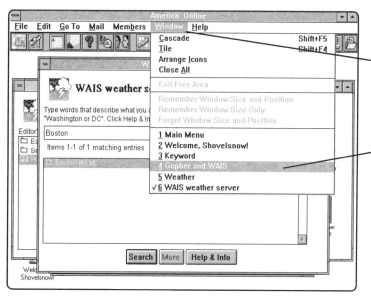

**1. Click** on **Window** in the menu bar. A pull-down menu will appear.

**2. Click** on **Gopher and WAIS.** The Gopher and WAIS dialog box will appear.

## EXPLORING ANOTHER ROAD

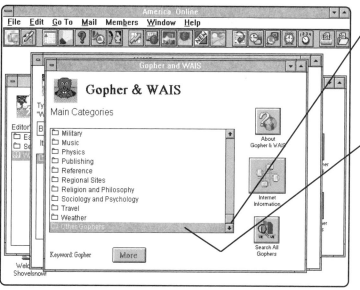

**1. Click repeatedly** on the ↓ **to scroll down** to the bottom of the list of categories.

**2. Click twice** on **Other Gophers**. The Other Gophers dialog box will appear.

This looks like a friendly road!

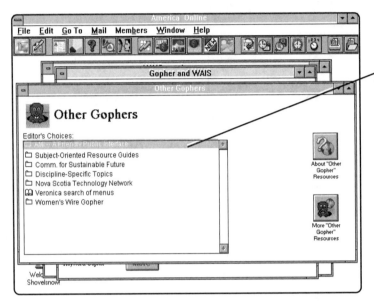

3. **Click twice** on **AMI — A Friendly Public Interface**. The AMI — A Friendly Public Interface dialog box will appear.

How about some entertainment?

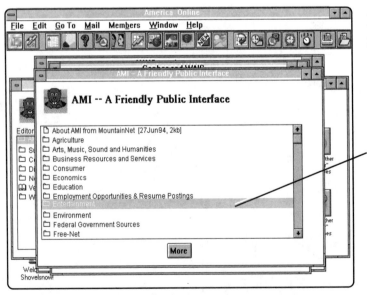

4. **Click twice** on **Entertainment**. The Entertainment dialog box will appear.

What could be more enter-taining than fun and games?

5. **Click twice** on **Fun & Games.** The Fun & Games dialog box will appear.

How about a trip to the movies?

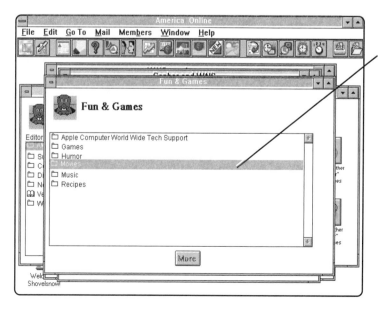

6. **Click twice** on **Movies.** The Movies dialog box will appear.

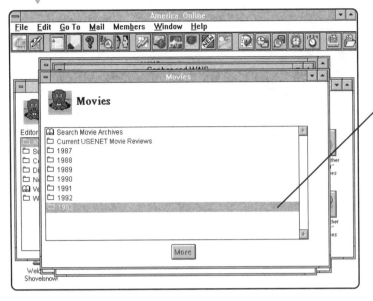

The Movies dialog box lets you choose the year the movie was released.

**7. Click twice** on **1993**. The 1993 dialog box should appear. Oops — an error message!

## Going Around Roadblocks

With millions of people using the Internet, you can expect to encounter a delay once in a while. So don't get discouraged by Internet error messages like this.

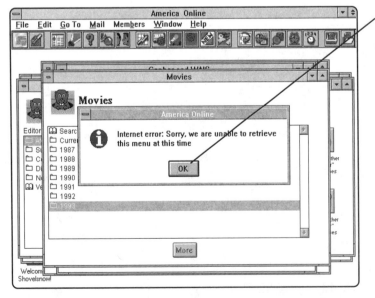

**1. Click** on **OK**. The America Online Internet error dialog box will close.

If you keep getting the error message, you can use the Window pull-down menu, like we did a few pages back, to take off down another road.

For this example, let's assume that we waited a minute and clicked twice on 1993 again.

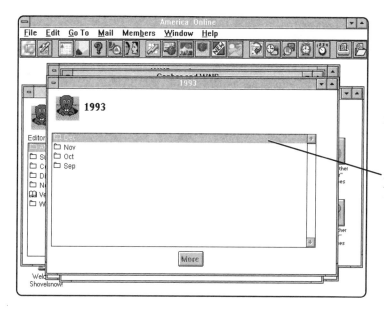

All right! We got through. The 1993 dialog box lists months during which movies were released.

2. **Click twice** on **Dec**. The Dec dialog box will appear.

3. **Click twice** on **GRUMPY OLD MEN.** The GRUMPY OLD MEN dialog box will appear.

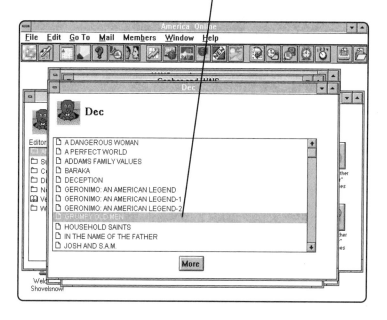

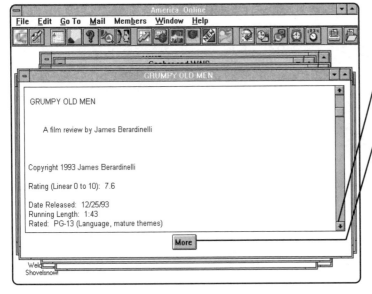

This is just the beginning of the movie review.

**4. Click repeatedly** on the **↓ to scroll down** the file.

5. **Click** on **More**, if needed, to view the rest of the file.

If you want to save or print the file, see the section "Saving a File" or "Printing a File," earlier in this chapter.

## CHANGING THE VIEW

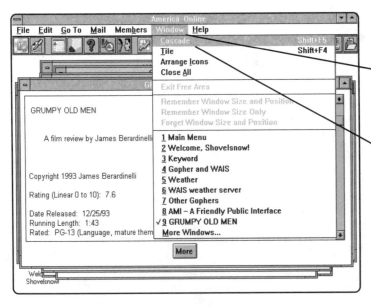

If the clutter of past dialog boxes is spoiling your view, you can change it.

1. **Click** on **Window** in the menu bar. A pull-down menu will appear.

2. **Click** on **Cascade.** The gopher dialog boxes will be staggered so that you can see all of their titles.

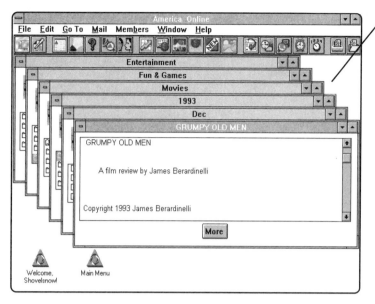

❖ The cascade view here shows all the dialog boxes you've opened so far in your current gopher tour, except for any that you may have closed along the way.

## GOING BACK TO A FAMILIAR INTERSECTION AGAIN

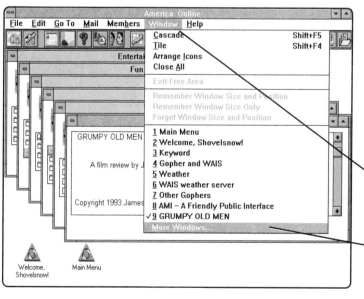

The Window pull-down menu has room to keep track of only a few of the gopher dialog boxes you've seen. Sometimes, to go back to a previous point, you have to use the More Windows choice.

1. **Click** on **Window** in the menu bar. A pull-down menu will appear.

2. **Click** on **More Windows.** The Select Window dialog box will appear.

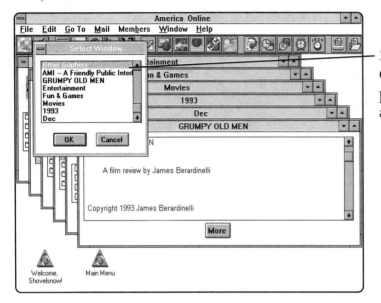

**3. Click twice** on **Other Gophers**. The Other Gophers dialog box will appear.

## MAXIMIZING A DIALOG BOX

You can click on the ▲ in the upper right corner of any dialog box to maximize it so that its contents are easier to see. In the example below, you will do this to more easily see an interesting icon we passed a while ago.

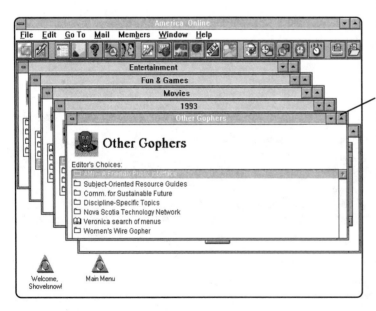

**1. Click** on the ▲ in the right corner of the Other Gophers dialog box. The dialog box will become maximized.

# VIEWING
# OTHER GOPHER RESOURCES

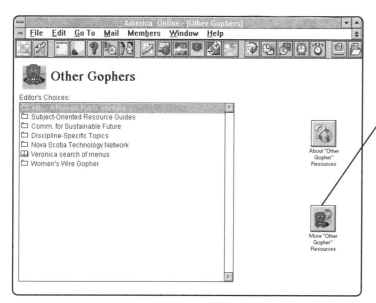

With the dialog box maximized, you can see the More "Other Gopher" Resources icon clearly.

**1. Click** on the **More "Other Gopher" Resources icon**. The More "Other Gopher" Resources dialog box will appear.

❖ As you can see from this list of choices, your trip could take you to computers all around the world and might go on forever! One gopher dialog box leads to another, then another, and before you know it, it's 2 o'clock in the morning!

❖ Some people call the random process of exploring that you have been doing in this chapter "surfing the Internet." Whether you call it that or "cruising the information highway," it doesn't matter. In either case, at some point, you've got to stop and go home!

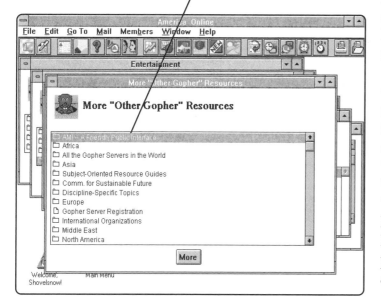

## SAYING GOOD-BYE TO GOPHER

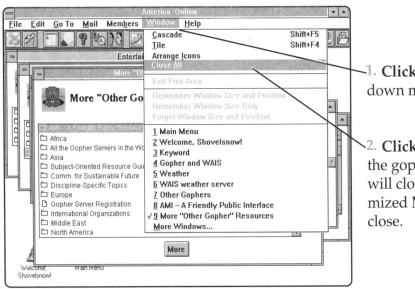

1. **Click** on **Window**. A pull-down menu will appear.

2. **Click** on **Close All.** All of the gopher dialog boxes will close, and the minimized Main Menu will close.

## SETTING THE AUTOMATIC SCROLLING OPTION

If you would prefer to have long files automatically scroll to the bottom, AOL allows you to set up this option. If you are not going to read a file online and plan to print or save it and read it later, this option speeds up the work.

1. **Click** on **Members** in the menu bar. A pull-down menu will appear.

2. **Click** on **Set Preferences**. The Preferences dialog box will appear.

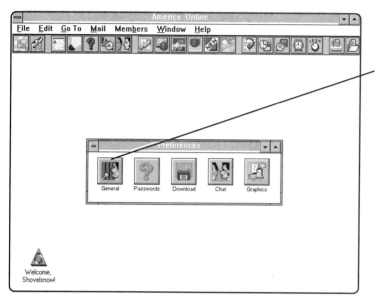

**3.** **Click** on the **General icon**. The General Preferences dialog box will appear.

**Note:** *If you want to read a file on your screen before you decide to print or save it, this option will drive you crazy.* When the automatic scrolling option is turned on, the lines of type whiz past you so fast that you can't read them.

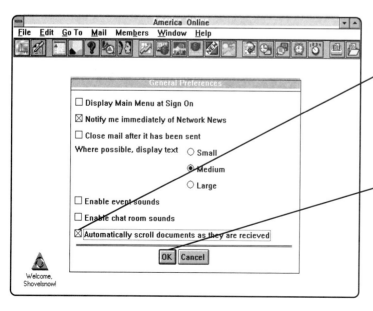

**4.** **Click** on **Automatically scroll documents as they are received** to put an ✕ in the box if it is not already there.

**5.** **Click** on **OK** (or Cancel). The Preferences dialog box will reappear.

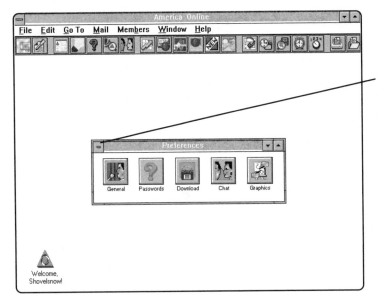

6. **Click twice** on the ☐ in the left corner of the Preferences dialog box. The dialog box will close.

## EXITING OR DISCONNECTING FROM AMERICA ONLINE

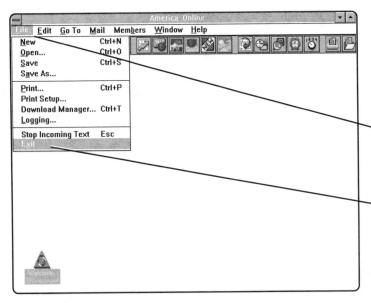

You can disconnect from AOL's online service and keep the America Online program running or exit the program completely.

1. **Click** on **File** in the menu bar. A pull-down menu will appear.

2. **Click** on **Exit**. An America Online dialog box will appear.

## Disconnecting Only

**1. Click** on **Yes.** You will be disconnected from the online service but the America Online program will still be running.

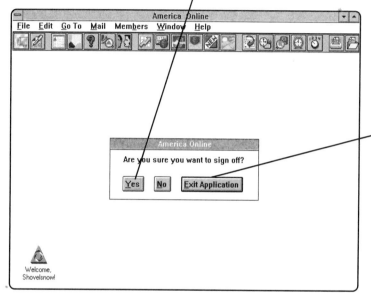

## Exiting Completely

**1. Click** on **Exit Application** to both disconnect and exit the America Online program. The Program Manager window will appear.

# Finding Business Opportunities Using Gopher and Veronica

The Internet contains a wealth of information useful to businesses both large and small. Much of this information comes from the U. S. government, and ranges from census statistics tables to text files that tell you about commercial prospects in the U.S. and abroad. In addition, you can find business opportunities on the Internet itself. In this chapter, you will:

❖ Use Gopher to find information that can help your business

## OPENING GOPHER

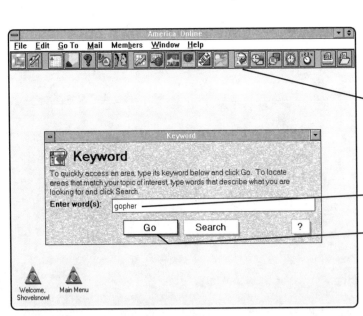

1. **Sign on to America Online** if you haven't already done so **and click** on the ▼s of both the Welcome screen and Main Menu to minimize them.

2. **Click** on the **Keyword icon** in the toolbar. The Keyword dialog box will appear.

3. **Type gopher**.

4. **Click** on **Go**. The Gopher & WAIS dialog box will appear.

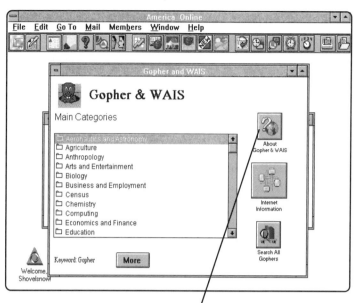

Gopher is named after the mascot of the University of Minnesota, where the Gopher system was developed. WAIS, pronounced "ways," is short for *Wide Area Information Server*. Gopher and WAIS are programs that allow you to search through huge amounts of information. They are like library card catalogs that keep track of information and where it is located.

## LEARNING ABOUT GOPHER AND WAIS

1. **Click** on the **About Gopher & WAIS icon**. The Help: Gopher and WAIS dialog box will appear.

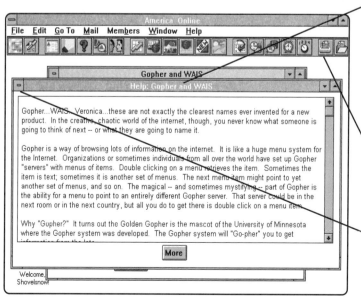

❖ This dialog box gives you background on Gopher, WAIS, and Veronica, all of which are programs you use to find information on the Internet.

2. **Click** on the **Print icon** in the toolbar. When the Print dialog box appears, **click** on **OK**. The file will print.

3. **Click twice** on the **Control menu box** (⊟) on the left of the title bar to close the dialog box. The Gopher and WAIS dialog box will reappear.

## BEGINNING AN INFORMATION SEARCH

The first step in a productive information search is reviewing your options and deciding where to begin. This is the heart of an effective search. Take a moment to scroll through the categories listed in the Gopher and WAIS dialog box. As you will see, the categories you can investigate range from Aerospace and Astronomy to Weather. Each category is like an information tree with hundreds of branches. Each branch gives you a different perspective on the topic and leads to additional choices that narrow the perspective even more. It's not possible within the confines of this chapter (or even this book) to take you through every single source of business information on the Internet. This chapter is meant to give you a feel for the possibilities and introduce you to the process of searching.

In this section, you'll go to the Economics and Finance category to start a search.

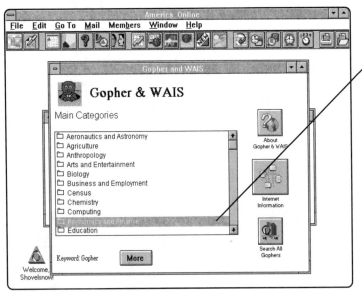

1. **Click twice** on **Economics and Finance**. A dialog box will appear with the Editor's Choices of the most popular Economics and Finance categories.

The file folder (📁) to the left of Economics and Finance means that another menu of choices will open when you click on the selection.

The Editor's Choices are chosen by folks at America Online. The list may change as certain Gophers are phased in or out or other interesting resources appear. You'll find as you go through the examples in this chapter that sources can change overnight on the Internet. Sources that we show in the chapter may not exist when you do your search. Other sources may appear on your screen that we don't show. Remember, no one "owns" or manages the Internet. It really is a wild child growing before our eyes. But that's part of its charm.

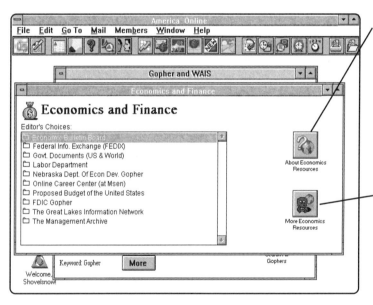

2. **Click** on the **About Economics Resources icon** to get a short description of the sources that are listed. Close the description box by **clicking twice** on the **Control menu box** (⊟) on the left of the title bar.

3. **Click** on the **More Economics Resources** icon for a more extensive listing that also includes the Editor's Choices. The More Economics Resources dialog box will appear.

## Narrowing the Search

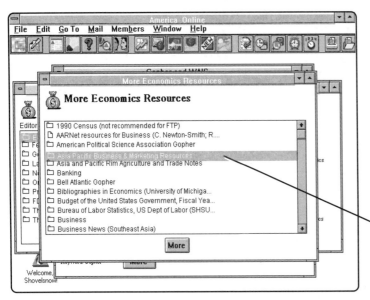

Now that you have the more complete list of Economic and Finance topics, scroll through the list to get an idea of the scope of information. In this section, you'll narrow the search by going to Asia Pacific Business and Marketing Resources.

1. **Click twice** on **Asia Pacific Business & Marketing Resources**. A dialog box will appear.

(You'll see lots of interesting choices as you proceed through this chapter, and at some point you should go back and spend some time exploring them. Fortunes have been made based on a serendipitous discovery of a bit of information!)

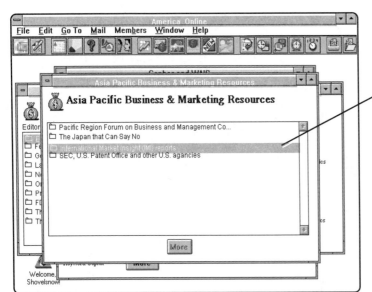

Notice that there are even more specific topics within this dialog box.

2. **Click twice** on **International Marketing Insight (IMI) Reports**. A dialog box will appear with more choices.

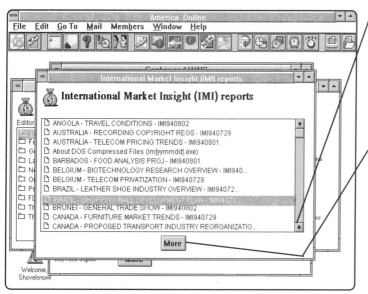

**3.** **Click repeatedly** on the ⬇ **to scroll down** the list. The list of reports changes regularly. The examples shown here will be replaced as new ones are written.

**4.** **Click** on **More** to see more choices.

**5.** **Click twice** on an item that interests you. In this example, it is Brazil - Shopping Mall Development Plan. The document icon (🗋) to the left of this item means that you will see a text file when you click twice.

## READING A FILE

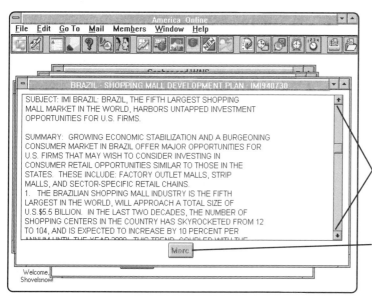

Even though you might have set your preferences in Chapter 14 to automatically scroll documents as they are received, only about 70 lines will be automatically scrolled.

**1.** **Click repeatedly** on the ⬇ or ⬆ to scroll through the file.

**2.** **Click** on **More** to see the rest of the file if all of it did not appear.

## SAVING A FILE

Text like this report can be saved or printed. If there's a More button at the bottom of its dialog box, click on it and scroll down to be sure that you have the whole file.

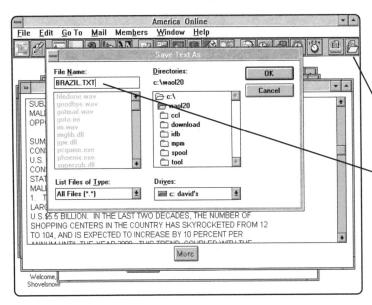

1. **Click** on the **Save icon** in the toolbar. The Save Text As dialog box will appear.

2. **Type** a **name, a dot, and the extension txt** to identify it as a text file.

3. **Click** on **OK**. In this example, the file will be copied to the C:\WAOL20 directory.

## TRYING A NEW SOURCE

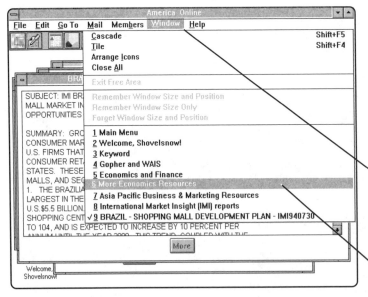

If you don't want to look at other information in the Market Insight Reports, you can go back to the More Economic Resources dialog box to find another information source.

1. **Click** on **Window** in the menu bar. A pull-down menu will appear, showing all open windows.

2. **Click** on **More Economics Resources**. The dialog box will reappear.

# CHECKING ON BANKING INFORMATION

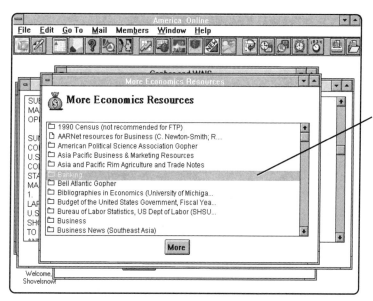

1. **Click twice** on **Banking.** The Banking dialog box will appear.

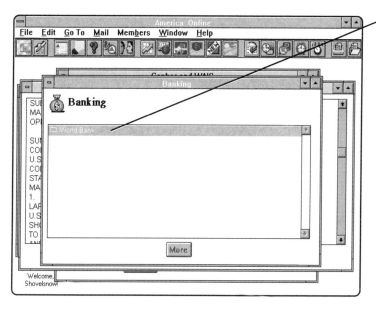

2. **Click twice** on **World Bank**. The World Bank dialog box will appear.

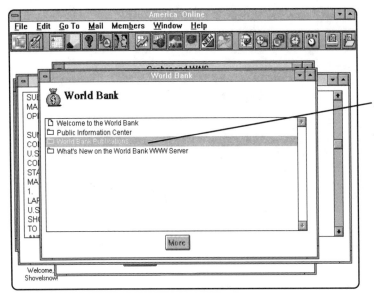

**3. Click twice** on **World Bank Publications**. The World Bank Publications dialog box will appear.

The third item in this example has an open-book symbol (📖) to its left. This means that clicking on this choice will open a WAIS search program. WAIS lets you search through an entire database (in this case, the World Bank's publications catalog) using keywords.

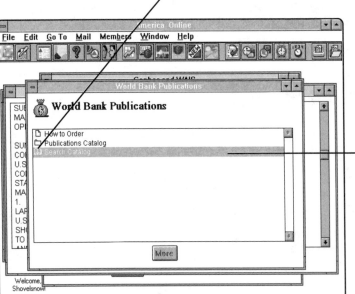

**4. Click twice** on **Search Catalog**. The Search Catalog dialog box will appear.

## SEARCHING WITH WAIS

When you do a WAIS search, you type a word (or words) for WAIS to look for. WAIS will look for the word in the database and give you a list of the files the word is in. If you misspell the word, WAIS will search for the misspelled version. It's only a computer, remember, and it does *exactly* what it is told.

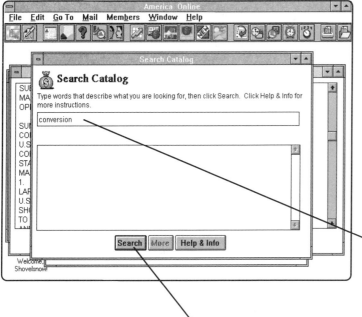

In this example, we'll search for information on economic conversion.

1. **Type Conversion**. Searches aren't case-sensitive, so it doesn't matter whether you use capitals.

2. **Click** on **Search**. A list of files that contain the word "conversion" will appear. (For more information on searching, see the section entitled "Refining your search with 'and,' 'or,' and 'but not,'" in Chapter 10).

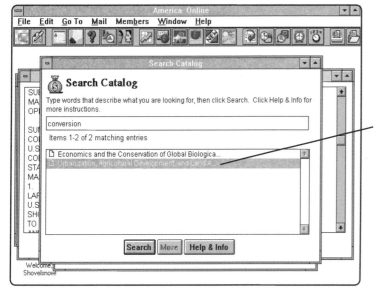

3. **Click twice** on **Urbanization, Agricultural Development, and Land**. The Urbanization, Agricultural Development, and Land dialog box will appear.

## Viewing the Search Results

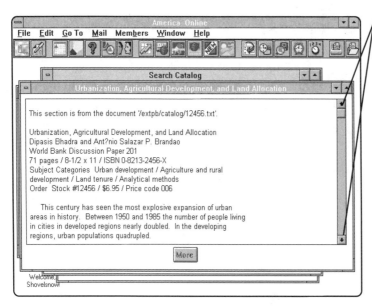

This section is from the document '/extpb/catalog/12456.txt'.

Urbanization, Agricultural Development, and Land Allocation
Dipasis Bhadra and Ant?nio Salazar P. Brandao
World Bank Discussion Paper 201
71 pages / 8-1/2 x 11 / ISBN 0-8213-2456-X
Subject Categories  Urban development / Agriculture and rural
development / Land tenure / Analytical methods
Order  Stock #12456 / $6.95 / Price code 006

This century has seen the most explosive expansion of urban
areas in history.  Between 1950 and 1985 the number of people living
in cities in developed regions nearly doubled.  In the developing
regions, urban populations quadrupled.

1. **Click repeatedly** on the ⬆ or ⬇ to scroll through the file. The file can be printed or saved, as shown earlier in this chapter.

Remember to check that you have the whole file before you print or save.

**Tip:** When the More button is grayed out, you have the entire file.

## CLOSING DIALOG BOXES

There's a limit to the number of gopher dialog boxes AOL lets you keep open at one time. If you reach the limit, an error message will ask you to close them. So let's close ones you've opened so far to avoid this problem.

involves conversion of agricultural land to nonagricultural uses.
Whether or not the reasons are economically sound, governments tend
to respond with interventions in land markets to stop or slow
conversion of land to urban use.

This paper reviews the literature on urbanization and
agricultural development and discusses the role of government in
conversion.  After a brief overview, the authors examine the links
between economic development, urbanization, and the economics of city
growth.  They also review the effects of urban development on
agriculture and consider the rationale and effect of government
intercession.

In reviewing the relevant literature, the authors build an
analytical framework for the evaluation of land allocation policies.

1. **Click twice** on the **Control menu boxes** (⊟) in the upper-left corner of each open dialog box to close them until you're back at **Gopher and WAIS** (see top of next page).

# EXPLORING OTHER AVENUES

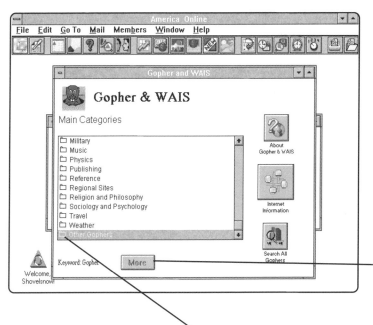

In this section, we'll try a less direct route to some business sources than we took earlier in the chapter. This will show you some "out-of-the-way" items and how to find them yourself.

If you've been following along, you'll be at the Gopher and WAIS dialog box.

1. **Click** on **More** for more choices, and then **scroll to** the **end** of the list.

2. **Click twice** on **Other Gophers**. The Other Gophers dialog box will appear.

3. **Click twice** on **Discipline-Specific Topics**. The Discipline-Specific Topics dialog box will appear.

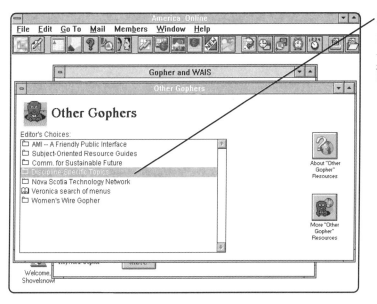

**4. Click twice** on **Clearinghouse for Subject-Oriented Internet Resour...** The Clearinghouse for Subject-Oriented Internet Resource Guides dialog box will appear.

❖ The Clearinghouse for Subject-Oriented Internet Resource Guides is maintained by the University of Michigan's School for Information and Library Studies. It contains guides to Internet resources compiled by professional information managers (a.k.a. librarians). Some of the guides are short enough to read (and save or print) by using Gopher.

**5. Click twice** on **Guides on the Social Sciences**. The Guides on the Social Sciences dialog box will appear.

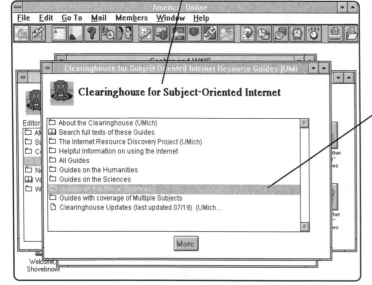

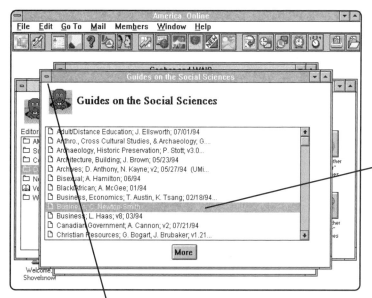

As you can see, there are three separate guides to business resources in this example. The first is by Austin & Tsang. The second is by Newton-Smith, and the third by Haas.

6. **Click twice** on the **Newton-Smith guide**. This is the shortest one, and it will give you a flavor for these resources. It contains information on electronic meetings, newsgroups, electronic journals, and databases that may be of interest. (Newsgroups are a great source of business information on the latest trends and what people are looking for in a wide variety of topics.)

The Austin & Tsang guide to government business information on the Internet is much longer. The Haas guide is the longest and is divided into sections ("General," "Economics," etc.).

You can start to read these guides by clicking twice on their titles. However, because of their length, you probably will not be able to receive the entire guide before getting an error message and running up online costs. (FTP, soon to be available through AOL's Internet Expert Connection, is the most efficient way to obtain lengthy files.)

7. **Click twice** on the **Control menu boxes** (⊟) in the upper-left corner of *each* open dialog box until you return to the Discipline-Specific Topics dialog box.

## FINDING INTERNET BUSINESSES

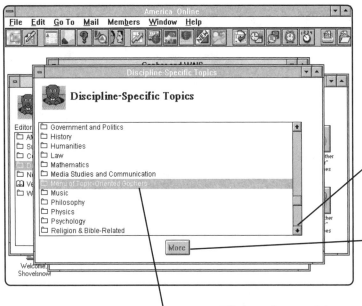

The Internet is already home to many businesses. This section will show you a couple of them and may give you some ideas for your own enterprise.

1. **Click repeatedly** on the ⬇ to **scroll down** the list.

2. **Click** on **More** to view more choices.

3. **Click twice** on **Menu of Topic-Oriented Gophers**. The Menu of Topic-Oriented Gophers dialog box will appear.

Several Gophers geared to businesses and commercial use of the Internet can be found by using this route.

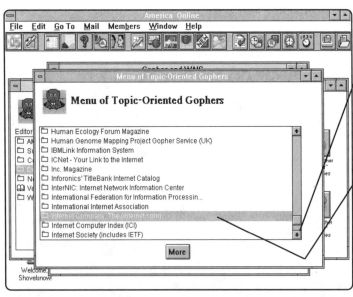

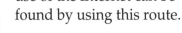

4. **Click repeatedly** on the ⬇ to **scroll down** the list.

5. **Click** on **More** to view more choices.

6. **Click twice** on **Internet Company, The (internet. com)**. The Internet Company, The (internet.com) dialog box will appear.

The Internet Company is an example of several enterprises started on the Internet in the past few years specifically to help businesses take advantage of the Internet's potential.

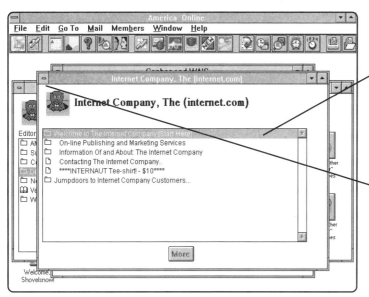

**7. Click twice** on **Welcome to the Internet Company (start here)** if you want to read information about this business.

**8. Click twice** on the **Control menu boxes** (⊟) to close any open dialog boxes until the Menu of Topic-Oriented Gophers dialog box reappears.

## EXPLORING AN "INTERNET MALL"

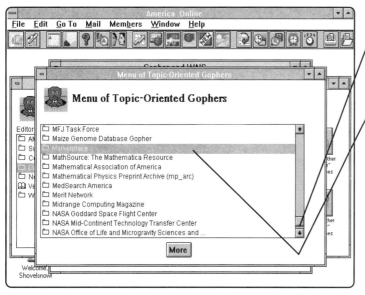

**1. Click repeatedly** on the ⬇ to **scroll down** the list.

**2. Click twice** on **Marketplace**. The Marketplace dialog box will appear.

Marketplace is another example of an Internet business started to help other businesses on the net. (Many frequent Internet users call it simply "the net.")

3. **Click twice** on **Complete Information on Cyberspace.** The Complete Information on Cyberspace dialog box will appear. This title changes often and may not be worded the way it is shown here.

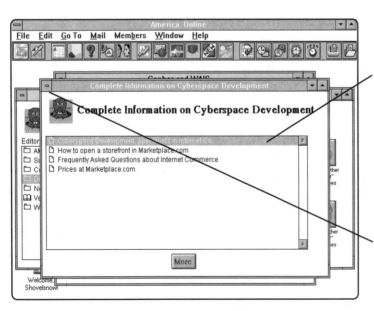

4. **Click twice** on **any topic** if you want to find out more about these services.

5. **Click twice** on the **Control menu boxes** (⊟) in the upper-left corner of *each* open dialog box until you return to the Gopher and WAIS dialog box.

# USING VERONICA
# TO SEARCH ALL GOPHERS

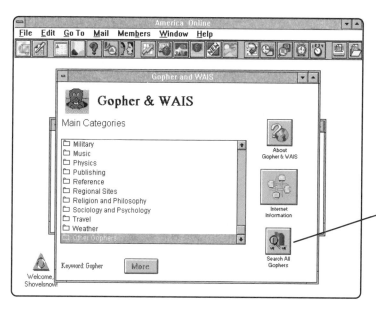

While WAIS searches for words contained in files, Veronica searches for words in Gopher menus. Both use keywords as the basis for the search. Keyword searches look for words that are "key," or central, to the topic being researched.

1. **Click** on **Search All Gophers**. The Search all Gophers with Veronica dialog box will appear.

2. **Type business tax**.

3. **Click** on **Search**. After a short wait, a list like the one in this example will appear.

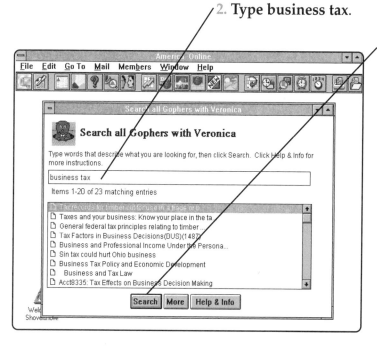

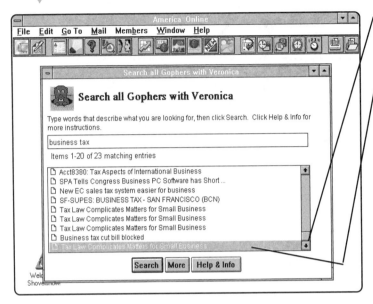

**4.** **Click repeatedly** on the ↓ to scroll **to the bottom** of the list of choices.

**5.** **Click twice** on **Tax Law Complicates Matters for Small Business.** The Tax Law Complicates Matters for Small Business dialog box will appear.

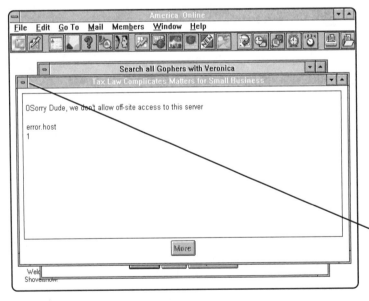

Apparently this document, whatever it might be, is on a computer to which "outsiders" do not have access. (You may get a slightly different error message when you try.) Veronica found what we asked for, but it's not something helpful.

Let's try again.

**6.** **Click twice** on the **Control menu box** (▭) to close this window and return to the Search All Gophers with Veronica dialog box.

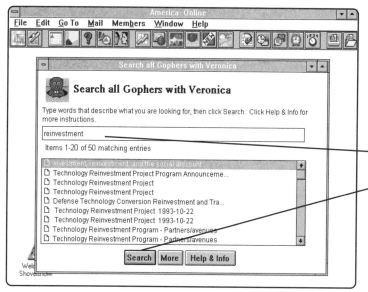

## Trying Again

1. **Click** to the **right** of "business tax" to set the cursor and **repeatedly press** the **Backspace key** to erase it.

2. **Type reinvestment**.

3. **Click** on **Search**. A list of sources will appear.

From the many repeat choices here, it should be apparent that keyword searching using Veronica to search Gopher menus is a little like a game of chance. Sometimes you win, sometimes you lose.

You'll find that many things on the Internet are put into Gophers for the convenience of the people using the computer the gopher is running on. They're not always there because the items might be of interest or useful to everyone who has access to the Internet.

Remember that the other tool for using keyword searches, WAIS, indexes specific computers and files that have been selected because of their potential usefulness. Because of this, keyword searches using a WAIS are usually more productive than keyword searches using Veronica. In either case, though, you need to be persistent — keep trying.

## REVIEWING KEYWORD SEARCH

❖ Choose the keyword carefully. Get to know the terminology related to the topic. General words usually don't work as well as specific terms do.

❖ Use the * character when a term can have several endings. For example, type divers* to search for "diversity," "diversify," and "diversification."

❖ Use words such as "and," "or," and "but not" to expand or limit your search.

❖ Keep trying. With thousands of computers on the net, you're bound to have to do some sifting.

## CLOSING ALL OPEN WINDOWS

At this point, you will have gained an understanding of how Gopher searches work and a little about the wealth of business information found on the Internet. You can continue to explore, or close all open windows.

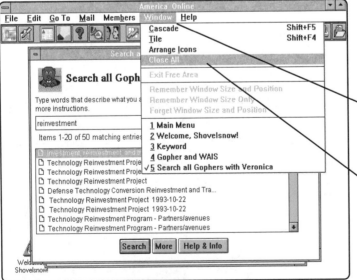

1. **Click** on **Window** in the menu bar. A pull-down menu will appear.

2. **Click** on **Close All**. All open windows will close, and the Welcome window will be reduced to an icon at the bottom of your screen.

### CHAPTER 16

# Researching A Term Paper

AOL's Internet Gopher, with WAIS and Veronica keyword search features, is a great way to find term paper information. Gopher is a huge Internet menu system, a sort of table of contents. WAIS can be described as an index to certain computers on the Internet. Another search feature, Veronica, can be helpful when searching for general topics. Gopher should not be used as your only source nor as a substitute for periodical indexes and books. However, it offers an opportunity to develop unique reports by using valuable sources of information and ideas that might not show up in a traditional library collection. You will notice that this chapter and Chapter 15 deal with different topics, but much of the search process is the same. We recommend that you go through both to help sharpen your search skills. In this chapter, you will do the following:

❖ Learn how to use Gopher to find information that could help you get an "A"

## OPENING GOPHER

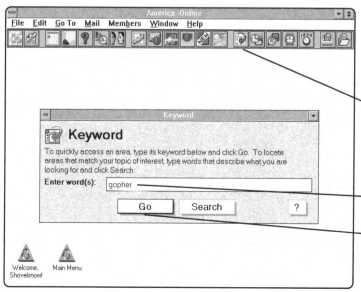

1. **Sign on to America Online** if you haven't already done so and **click** on the ▼s of both the Welcome screen and Main Menu to minimize them.

2. **Click** on the **Keyword icon** in the toolbar. The Keyword dialog box will appear.

3. **Type gopher**.

4. **Click** on **Go**. The Gopher & WAIS dialog box will appear.

❖ The Main Categories listed in this dialog box were selected by the AOL Internet team. They are a good starting point for a search.

## LEARNING BY EXAMPLE

Searching for term paper information using Gopher can be maddening because the available information keeps changing all the time. That's because the Internet is a dynamic, unregulated system. By its very nature, it is being upgraded and changed on an almost moment-to-moment basis.

The best way to use this chapter is to think of it as *learning by example*. Just follow the steps, but recognize that some of the steps may yield different results than the ones shown here. The idea is to get a feel for the Gopher search process so that you can conduct a search on your own topic.

## FINDING YOUR FIRST FILE

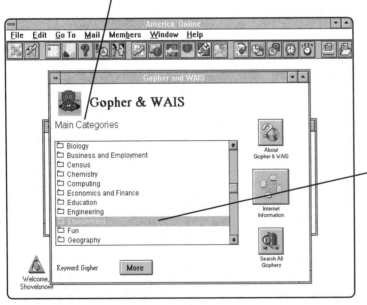

In this section, we used "sustainable development" (the development of renewable energy, food sources, and industries for the future) as our example for this term paper topic.

1. **Click twice** on **Environment**. The Environment dialog box will appear.

## Reading Topic Descriptions

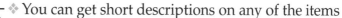

❖ You can get short descriptions on any of the items listed in the Editor's Choice by clicking on the About Environment Resources icon. After you have reviewed the descriptions, you can close the descriptions dialog box by clicking twice on the Control menu box (▭) in the left corner of the title bar.

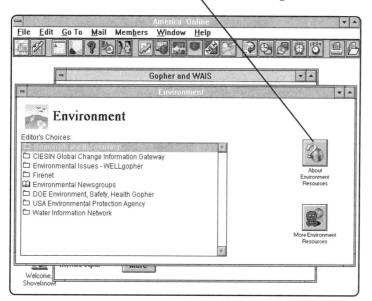

❖ You will see many interesting choices as you proceed through this chapter, and at some point you might want to go back and spend some time exploring them.

❖ Gopher can be an excellent source of ideas if you have to develop your own term paper topic, project, or classroom discussion.

## Reading a File Online

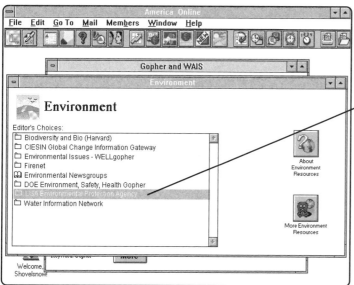

1. **Click twice** on **USA Environmental Protection Agency**. The USA Environmental Protection Agency dialog box will appear.

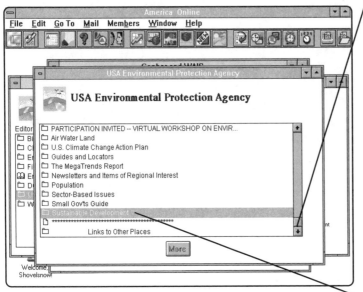

**2.** **Click repeatedly** on the ⬇ to **scroll down** the list of topics.

**3.** **Click twice** on **Sustainable Development**. The Sustainable Development dialog box will appear.

**4.** **Click twice** on **Workshop Report: Sustainable Architecture**. The Workshop Report: Sustainable Architecture dialog box will appear.

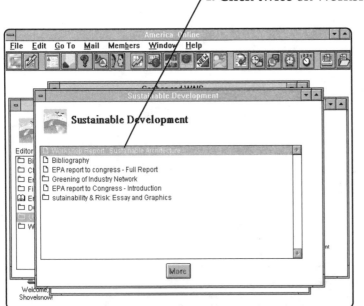

**5. Click repeatedly** on the ⬇ to **scroll down** the file to read the text.

**6. Click** on **More** to read the rest of the file. When the More button is grayed out, it means that the entire file is in your computer's memory and can be saved to your hard drive or to a disk.

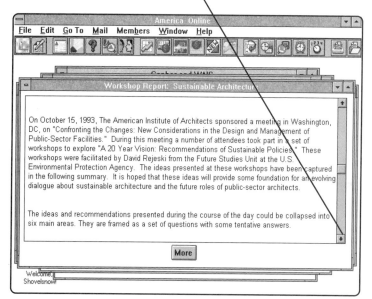

## SAVING A FILE

Since most of the files you find by using Gopher tend to be lengthy, saving the file will save you online time. Once the file has been saved, you can read and print it off-line at your leisure.

**1. Click** on the **Save icon** in the toolbar. The Save As dialog box will appear.

**2. Type** a **name** for the file in the File Name text box.

**3. Click** on **OK**. The dialog box will close. The file will be copied to the directory shown in the Save As dialog box.

**4. Click twice** on the ⊟ in the left corner of the Workshop Report title bar. The dialog box will close.

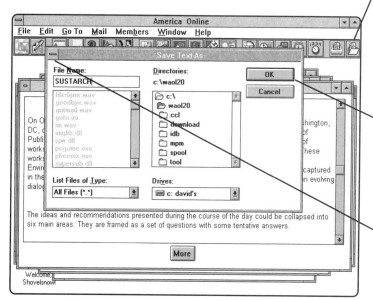

# REACHING A DEAD END

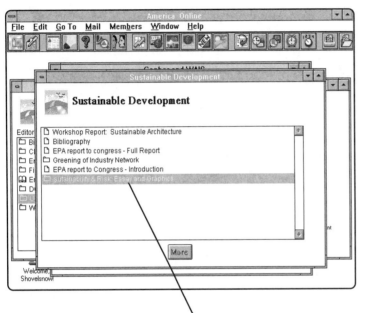

Items available on Gopher menus change over time. This can happen because the information changes or becomes out of date, a computer goes off-line, or the Gopher editors believe that other information might be more useful. This means that the Internet is full of shifting sands, potholes, and unexplained phenomena. In this example, you will experience a "dead end" through no fault of your own. The one illustrated here is typical.

1. **Click twice** on **sustainability and Risk: Essays and Graphics**. The Sustainability and Risk: Essays and Graphics dialog box will appear.

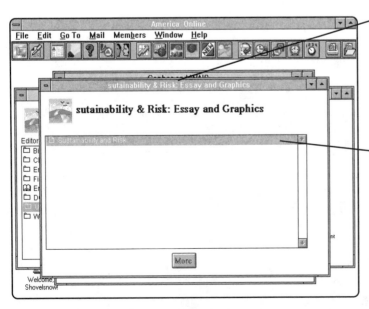

❖ This dialog box appears to have only one item in it! It might actually contain several graphics or executable files that aren't shown by the Gopher program.

2. **Click twice** on **Sustainability and Risk**. The Sustainability and Risk dialog box will appear.

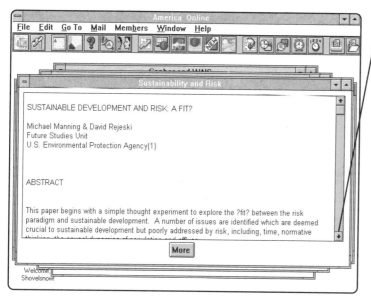

3. **Click repeatedly** on the ↓ to **scroll down** the file.

4. **Click** on **More** to view more of the file.

5. **Repeat steps 3** and **4** to view the entire file.

*Oops! An unexpected America Online dialog box appeared.*

The next screen illustrates a problem with lengthy files: Sometimes you can't get it all. If you save or print it, the last part is missing. In this case, we have the text but not all the references at the end.

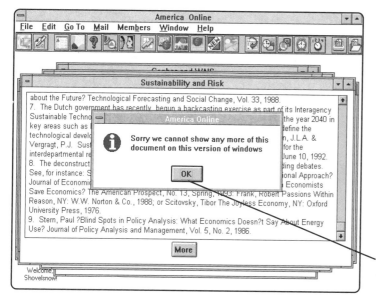

In a case like this, you have to decide whether you've received enough of the file for your purposes. Don't forget that you have to provide citations for your sources when you write a term paper. If you haven't received the data you need in order to cite the source, it might not be acceptable to your instructor.

6. **Click** on **OK**. The dialog box will close.

# PRINTING A FILE

1. **Click** on the **Print icon** on the toolbar. The Print dialog box will appear.

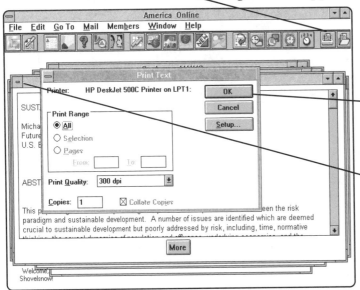

**Note**: This is a long file. Click on Cancel if you'd rather not print it.

2. **Click** on **OK**. The dialog box will close. The file will print.

3. **Click twice** on the **Control menu boxes** (⊟) of each of the dialog boxes you have visited to close them one at a time until the USA Environmental Protection Agency dialog box shown below appears.

# SEARCHING FROM GOPHER TO GOPHER

Going from Gopher to Gopher is a snap. The AOL program does the connection work for you!

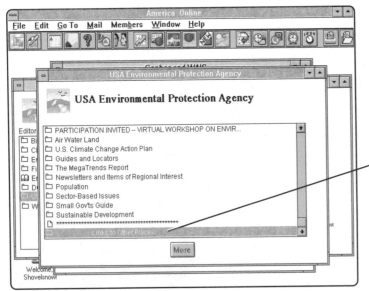

1. **Scroll down** the list and then **click twice** on **Links to Other Places**. The Links to Other Places dialog box will appear.

# Narrowing the Search

In this section, you will narrow the search to another Gopher containing a library of environmental information.

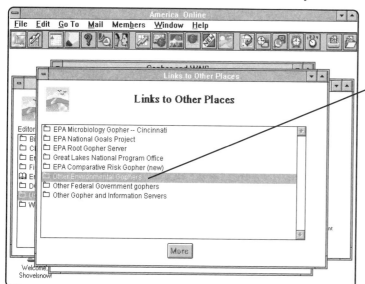

1. **Click twice** on **Other Environmental Gophers**. The Other Environmental Gophers dialog box will appear.

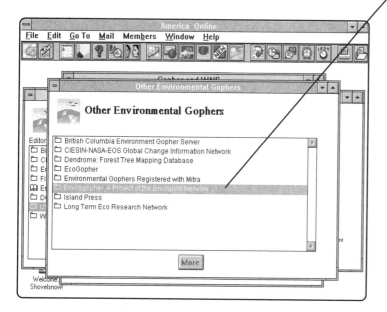

2. **Click twice** on **Envirogopher, a Project of the Envirolink Network**. The Envirogopher, a Project of the Envirolink Network dialog box will appear.

3. **Click twice** on **Enviroinformation — A Library of Environmental**. The Enviroinformation — A Library of Environmental Information dialog box will appear. (What a mouthful!)

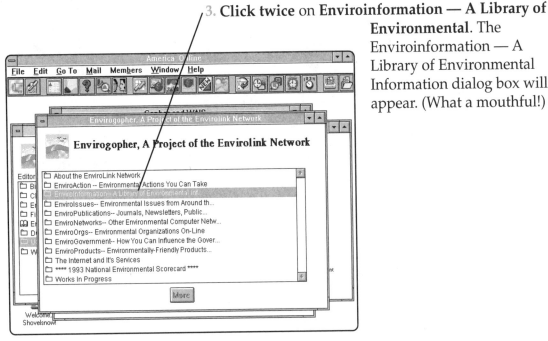

## CITING AN ELECTRONIC SOURCE

The sources you use in a term paper must be cited. There is a special format for citing electronic sources. In this example, we selected a report on a wind farm in Maine to illustrate how to cite an electronic reference.

1. **Click twice** on **Energy Info**. The Energy Info dialog box will appear.

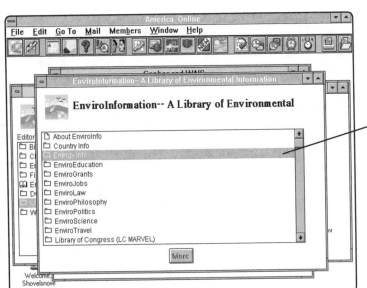

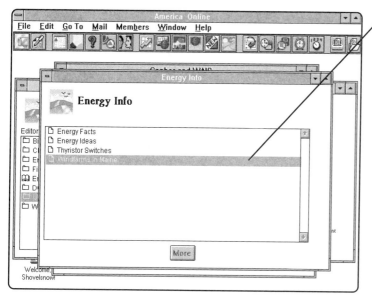

2. **Click twice** on **Windfarms in Maine**. The Windfarms in Maine dialog box will appear.

The citations for electronic sources should contain:

❖ The name of the author (individual or corporate)

❖ The date the source was published

❖ Enough information so the source can be located

Here's a sample citation for this article:

Gray, Tom (1993), "Endless Energy Starts Permit Process for Maine Windfarm." Available Gopher: Envirogopher\ Enviroinformation\ Energy Info\ Windfarms in Maine.

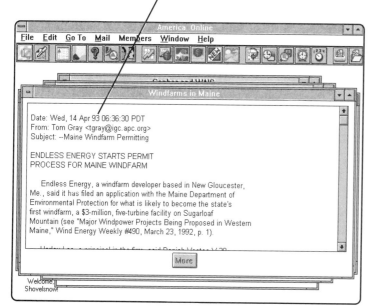

Check with your instructor *before writing your paper* to be sure that Gopher sources and the form of citation above are acceptable.

A useful guide to citing electronic sources is: *Electronic Style: A Guide to Citing Electronic Information*, by Xia Li and Nancy B. Crane (Westport, CT; Meckler, 1993).

## RETURNING TO HOME BASE

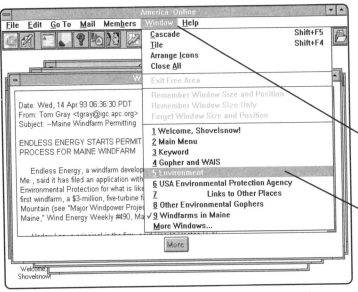

To quickly return to the original starting point in your Gopher search (or anywhere in between), the Window pull-down menu is the ticket.

**1. Click** on **Window** in the menu bar. A pull-down menu will appear.

**2. Click** on **Environment**. The Environment dialog box will appear. This dialog box was your starting point in the current search.

## READING A README FILE

In this section, you will view a README file in a Gopher dialog box. When you see a name like "README" or "About..." in a dialog box, it's a good idea to check it out. These files, usually written by the Gopher editor, give you more about what's behind the Gopher, or its contents.

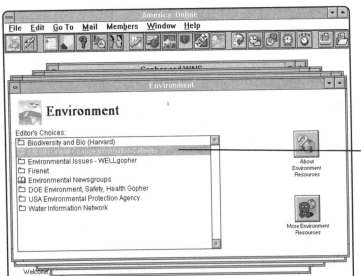

**1. Click twice** on **CIESIN Global Change Information Gateway**. The CIESIN Global Change Information Gateway dialog box will appear.

*CIESIN* (pronounced "season"), stands for Consortium for International Earth Science Information Network. It is a good example of one of many specialized information centers on the Internet that are trying to help manage the "information explosion."

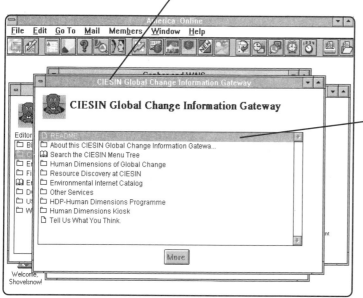

2. **Click twice** on README. The README dialog box will appear.

This README file is an excellent example of the *ever-changing nature of Gophers*. If you can't find our examples when you are following the steps in this book, the chances are that the file may be temporarily unavailable because the Gopher editor is making changes, as you can see in this example.

## Closing the README File

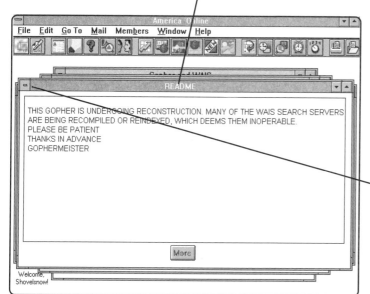

1. **Click** on the ⊟ in the left corner of the README title bar. The CIESIN Global Change Information Gateway dialog box will appear.

# SEARCHING WITH KEYWORDS USING WAIS

In this section, you will do a keyword search using WAIS. WAIS is short for Wide Area Information Server. WAIS is a program that searches through files on certain computers.

The search process is easy. You just give WAIS a keyword or string of keywords to search for. WAIS then lists all the files in which the word(s) occur. However, please note that WAIS searches for *exactly the word or words you specify, even if they're misspelled.*

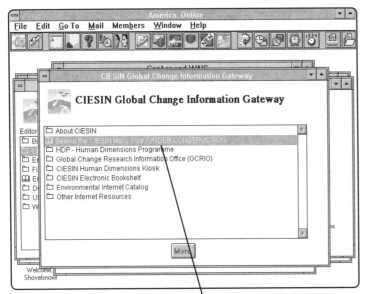

1. **Click twice** on **Search the CIESIN Menu Tree**. The Search the CIESIN Menu Tree dialog box will appear.

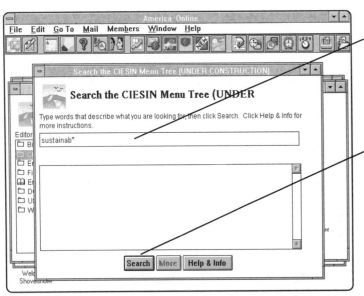

2. **Type sustainab\***. The asterisk (*) tells the WAIS program to search for any word that starts with "sustainab."

3. **Click** on **Search**. A list of files containing words starting with "sustainab" will appear.

Eureka! WAIS has found several files with the words "sustainable" and "sustainability" in them. Progress!

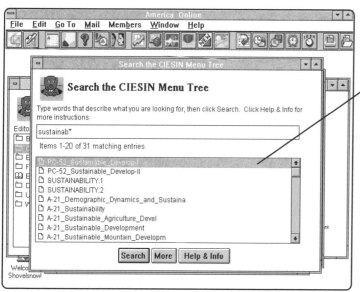

4. **Click twice** on **PC-52_Sustainable_Develop-I**. The PC-52_Sustainable_Develop-I dialog box will appear, containing the first file on the list. The file can be saved or printed if it looks like one you can use in your term paper.

## Closing Dialog Boxes

If you have too many dialog boxes open at a time, you will receive an AOL error message telling you to close some of them before going on. To avoid this interruption, it's a good idea to close each dialog box when you're finished with it.

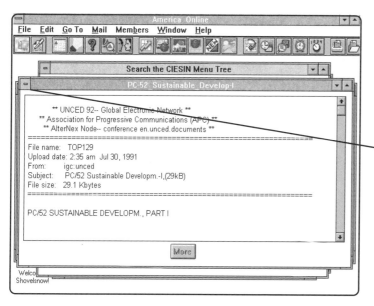

1. **Click twice** on the **Control menu boxes** (⊟) in the upper-left corner of the title bars of *each* open dialog box until the Gopher and WAIS dialog box pictured at the top of the next page appears.

# SEARCHING WITH KEYWORDS USING VERONICA

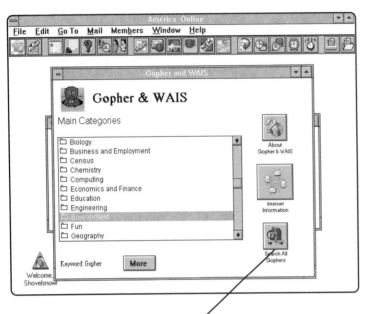

Both WAIS and Veronica are programs that search the Internet using keywords. The difference is that WAIS searches files on selected computers, and Veronica searches Gopher menus. Selecting a keyword that is neither too broad nor too limited is important to performing a good search. It is also helpful if you are familiar with the jargon, or "buzzwords," used by professionals in your topic area.

1. **Click** on **Search All Gophers**. The Search all Gophers with Veronica dialog box will appear.

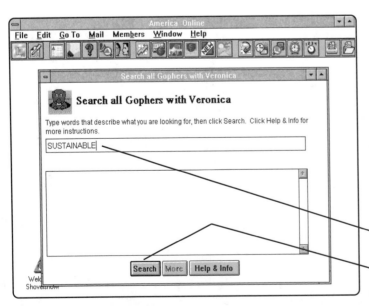

When you do a search in a library, there are standardized sets of words, called subject headings, that are used to classify the books and journal articles by topic. In contrast, *on the Internet, filenames, Gopher menus, etc. are not standardized.* Therefore, finding what you want can be tricky. Being lucky helps!

2. **Type sustainable**.

3. **Click** on **Search**. A list of menu items will appear.

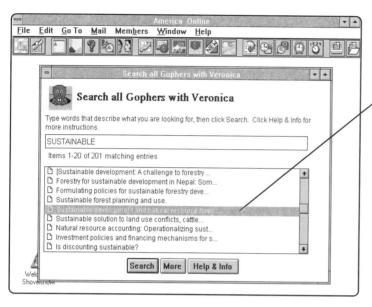

4. **Click repeatedly** on the ⬇ to **scroll down** the list of matching items.

5. **Click twice** on **Sustainable development and natural resource forecasting**. The Sustainable development and natural resource forecasting dialog box will appear.

## Finding an Abstract by Chance

Sometimes a menu item on a Gopher looks like just what you want for your term paper. However, when you open the file, it turns out to be something less than terrific in the sense that you can't immediately read, save, or print it. In this case, the item turned out to be an abstract. To get the full text of the article, you will have to find the periodical it refers to. This is not always an easy task. The next section has suggestions on how to get the full text of this article.

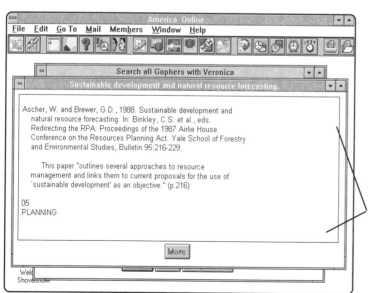

Notice that there is no scroll bar on this dialog box. This means that the complete text of this reference is shown on the screen.

# Getting the Information

There are several ways you can go about getting the full text of this paper, all of which take time:

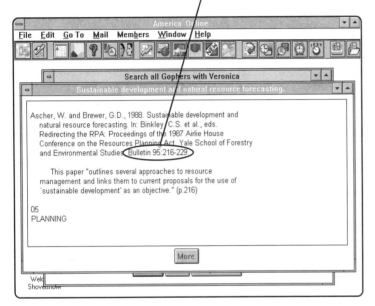

❖ Check your school's library to see if it receives the publication referred to.

❖ Telephone or write the Yale School of Forestry and Environmental Studies. With luck, you'll be able to connect with the editor of the *Bulletin,* who can help you get a copy.

❖ Ask your librarian about getting a copy through interlibrary loan.

## CLOSING MORE DIALOG BOXES

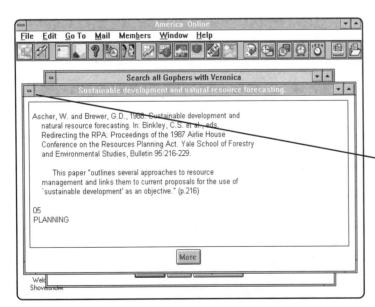

You can explore on your own the other items Veronica found. Let's go back to the Gopher and WAIS dialog box to try another way.

1. **Click twice** on the **Control Menu boxes** (⊟) of each open dialog box until the Gopher and WAIS dialog box appears.

# FINDING RESOURCE GUIDES

In this section, you will visit The Clearinghouse for Subject-Oriented Resource Guides, maintained by the University of Michigan's School of Information and Library Studies. It is an excellent starting point for a term paper search.

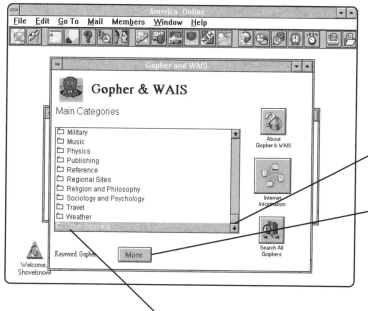

1. **Click repeatedly** on the ⬇ to **scroll down** the list.

2. **Click** on **More** to view more choices.

3. **Repeat steps 1 and 2** until you see the Other Gopher and Information Servers choice at the bottom of the list.

4. **Click twice** on **Other Gophers**. The Other Gophers dialog box will appear.

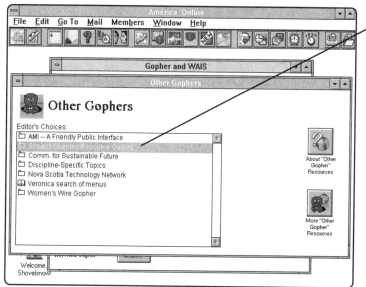

5. **Click twice** on **Subject-Oriented Resource Guides**. The Subject-Oriented Resource Guides dialog box will appear.

The Subject-Oriented Resource Guides are written by librarians. Some are short enough to read and save by using Gopher. (FTP, soon to be available through AOL's Expert Connection, is the most efficient way to obtain lengthy files over the Internet.)

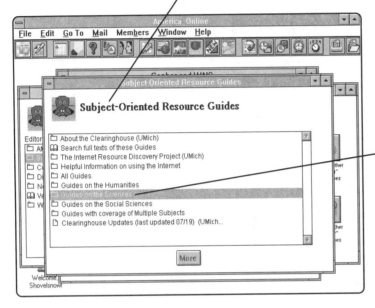

## Viewing a Guide

1. **Click twice** on **Guides to the Sciences**. The Guides to the Sciences dialog box will appear.

2. **Click repeatedly** on the ⬇ to **scroll down** the list of guides.

3. **Click** on **More** to view more choices.

4. **Continue to click repeatedly** on the ⬇ to **scroll down** until the items beginning with the letter "E" appear.

5. **Click twice** on **Ecology & Environmental Studies; L. Haas**. The Ecology & Environmental Studies; L. Haas dialog box will appear.

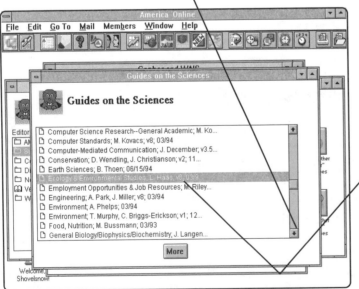

# Summing Up Resource Guides

❖ Resource guides, like the Haas guide shown here, will help you get the full range of information sources available from the Internet. These Internet sources range from mailing lists to newsgroups to Gophers to files on remote computers that you will soon be able to get by using Expert Connection.

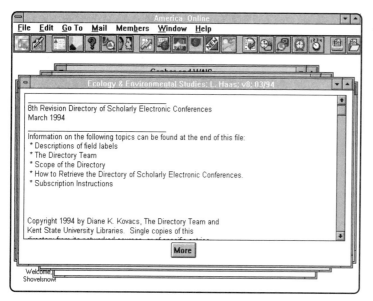

❖ This example, the Haas guide, is a relatively short guide to mailing lists (see Chapter 10 on how to sign up for a mailing list).

❖ Used in conjunction with the traditional book and periodical sources in your library, resource guides can give you an edge in almost any academic project.

❖ Before closing, you may want to review some of the other guides on your own. If not, go on to the next page to exit from America Online.

## EXITING FROM AOL

You can exit from AOL even if you have several open windows.

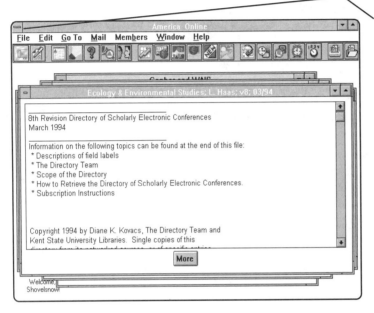

1. **Click twice** on the **Control menu box** (⊟) in the left corner of the America Online title bar. An AOL dialog box will appear.

2. **Click** on **Yes** to sign off but leave the AOL program running.

3. **Click** on **Exit Application** to disconnect, exit from the AOL program, and return to Program Manager.

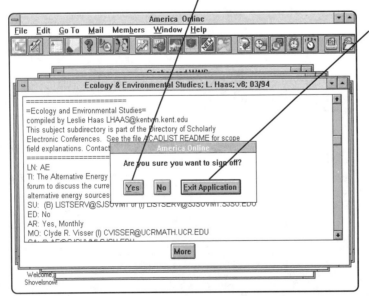

# Job Hunting on the Internet

If you're between jobs, dissatisfied with your present job, or just want to see how your job (and your salary) compare with others, the Internet offers you a variety of job information resources. You can use Gopher to tap into job databases, check their listings, and find services to post your resume to for employers to see. You can also join newsgroups that list job openings. (See Chapters 12 and 14 if you have not familiarized yourself with newsgroups and Gopher.) In this chapter, you will do the following:

❖ Get a guide to newsgroups that receive up-to-the minute job listings
❖ Use Gopher to find job-hunting resources

## OPENING GOPHER

1. **Sign on to America Online** if you haven't already done so and **click** on the ▼s of both the Welcome screen and Main Menu to minimize them.

2. **Click** on the **Keyword icon** in the toolbar. The Keyword dialog box will appear. (If you customized your Go To menu in Chapter 4, you can also go to Gopher by using that menu.)

3. **Type gopher**.

4. **Click** on **Go**. The Gopher and WAIS dialog box will appear.

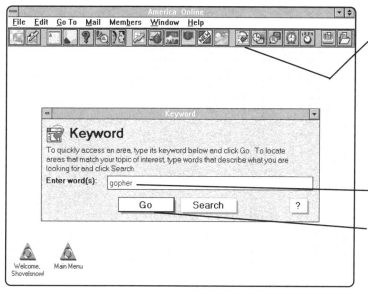

# BEGINNING YOUR SEARCH

AOL's Gopher has two routes to job information.
We'll start with the less obvious one.

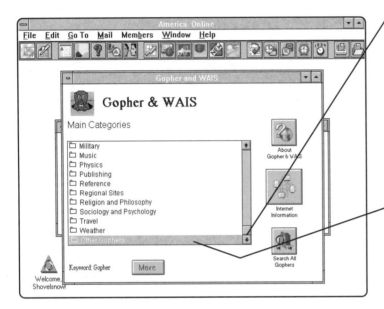

1. **Click repeatedly** on the
   ⬇ to **scroll down** the list of
   choices.

2. **Click** on **More** to view
   more choices.

3. **Repeat steps 1 and 2** to
   scroll to the end of the list.

4. **Click twice** on **Other
   Gophers.** The Other
   Gophers dialog box will
   appear.

5. **Click twice** on **AMI — A Friendly Public interface**. The AMI — A
   Friendly Public Interface
   dialog box will appear.

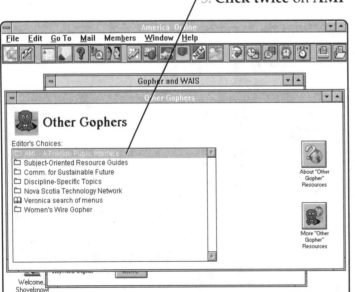

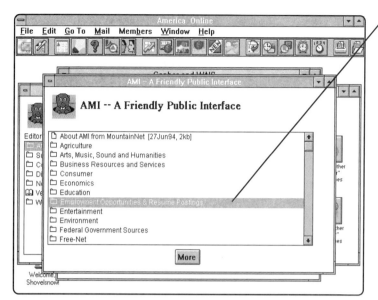

6. **Click twice** on **Employment Opportunities & Resume Postings**. The Employment Opportunities & Resume Postings dialog box will appear.

## GETTING A NEWSGROUP GUIDE

Many librarians have written guides to the Internet by subject (see "Finding Resource Guides," toward the end of Chapter 16). Margaret Riley's guide to job information includes the names of job-related newsgroups and is listed on this gopher menu.

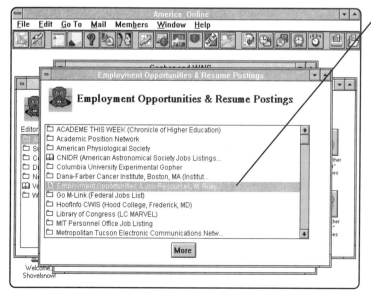

1. **Click twice** on **Employment Opportunities & Job Resources; M. Riley**. The Employment Opportunities & Job Resources; M. Riley dialog box will appear.

❖ The first part of the Riley guide lists newsgroups that feature job listings. If you try to join all newsgroups related to jobs (see Chapter 12), you'll find that there are too many. This list gives you specific names for those that are appropriate to your job search. You can cut down on online time by saving the file and reading it later (see below).

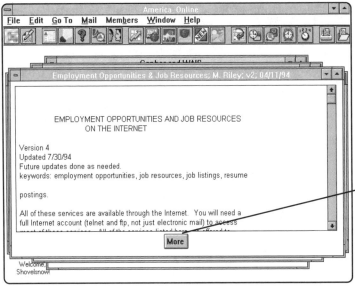

2. **Click** on **More** until it is grayed out, indicating that the whole file has been received.

**Note:** You may receive an error message indicating that no more of the file can be received. If you do, don't worry — the newsgroup information is in the first part of the file.

## Saving the Guide

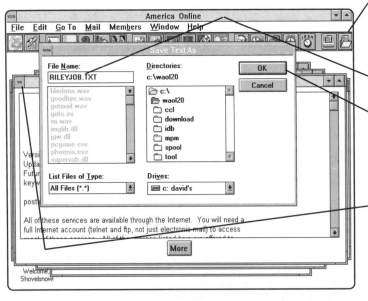

1. **Click** on the **Save icon** in the toolbar. The Save Text As dialog box will appear.

2. **Type** a **name** for the file.

3. **Click** on **OK**. The file will be saved to the c:\waol20 directory unless you have changed things.

4. **Click twice** on the **Control menu box** (▭) to close the open dialog box. The Employment Opportunities & Resume Postings dialog box will reappear.

## USING GOPHER TO "GO FER" JOBS

❖ Clicking twice on some of these choices leads to lists from individual employers and some to collections of job listings. In this example, we'll look at jobs at the Massachusetts Institute of Technology.

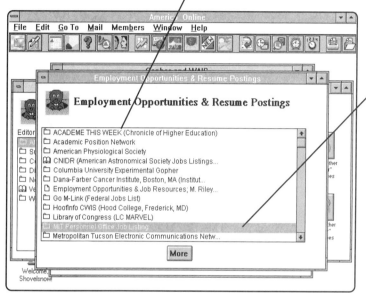

1. **Click twice** on **MIT Personnel Office Job Listing**. The MIT Personnel Office Job Listing dialog box will appear.

❖ This job Gopher is arranged by general job category and includes a general policy statement.

2. **Click twice** on **Personnel Employment Notice**. The Personnel Employment Notice dialog box will appear.

❖ Policy notices like this contain information you will need in order to apply for the jobs posted here. It's a good idea to save or print the file for future reference. Click on the Print and/or Save icon in the toolbar.

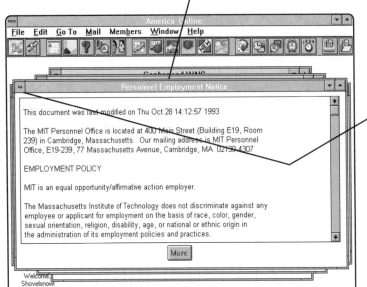

3. **Click twice** on the **Control menu box** (⊟) to close the dialog box. The MIT Personnel Office Job Listing dialog box will reappear.

## Viewing an Online Job Listing

Let's take a look at some of the jobs that our example, MIT, has open. Keep in mind that when you try this, the listings will be different from the ones shown here. The process, however, is the same for any employment posting on the Employment Opportunities and Resume Postings Gopher.

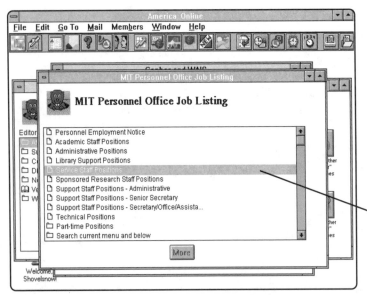

1. **Click twice** on **Service Staff Positions.** The Service Staff Positions dialog box will appear.

❖ When you're looking for a new job, don't limit yourself to the same environment in which you're now working. Just as there are jobs for welders at universities, there are jobs for people with academic backgrounds in commerce and industry.

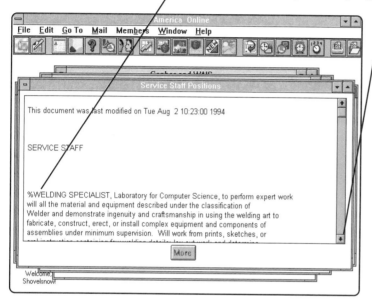

2. **Click repeatedly** on the ↓ **to read** about all the jobs listed in this file. If a job listing interests you, save or print the file and follow up later. The other Gophers for specific employers work the same way as this one. Feel free to explore on your own.

## SENDING YOUR RESUME TO AN ONLINE JOB SERVICE

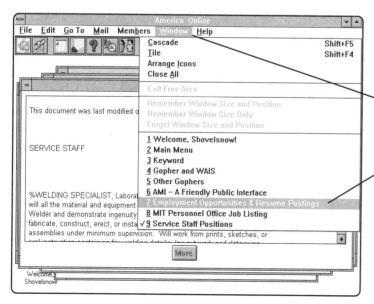

Let's find out how to post your own resume on the Internet:

1. **Click** on **Window** in the menu bar. A pull-down menu will appear.

2. **Click** on **Employment Opportunities & Resume Postings**. The Employment Opportunities & Resume Postings dialog box will appear.

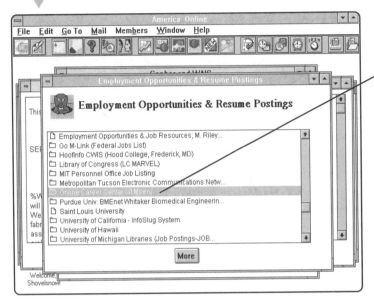

3. **Click repeatedly** on the ⬇ to **scroll down** the list.

4. **Click twice** on **Online Career Center (at MSEN)**. The Online Career Center (at MSEN) dialog box will appear.

❖ The Online Career Center is an example of a service that lists a wide range of jobs from a variety of employers. Services such as this often list jobs in several ways: by location, type of job, employer, etc.

5. **Click twice** on **About Online Career Center**. The About Online Career Center dialog box will appear.

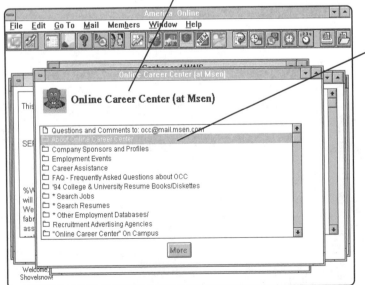

❖ These files will give you information about the Online Career Center.

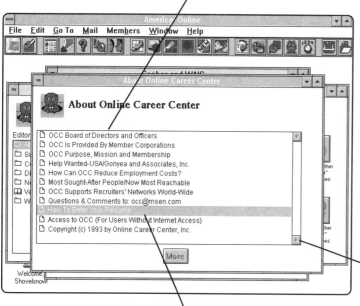

## Getting Directions

One of O.C.C.'s features is that you can e-mail your resume to them so that prospective employers will get a chance to see it. Here's how to get written instructions on how to e-mail your resume to the service.

1. **Click repeatedly** on the ⬇ to **scroll down** the list.

2. **Click Twice** on **How To Enter Your Resume**. The How To Enter your Resume dialog box will appear.

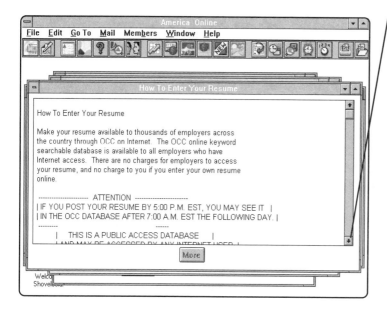

3. **Click repeatedly** on the ⬇ to read the file.

❖ If you e-mail your resume to the Online Career Center, they will keep it on their system for 90 days. Or for a $10 fee, you can mail a typed copy of your resume to the Center. The Center will then load it into its system and keep it online for six months.

## Printing the Directions

If you are planning on e-mailing your letter to the service, it is essential that you print this file, read it carefully, and follow the instructions. One of the most important criteria is that your resume must be typed in an ASCII format (e.g., a plain text file). By the way, AOL's Compose Mail program writes your message in a text format. If you don't have a text editor, you can compose your resume in the Compose Mail dialog box.

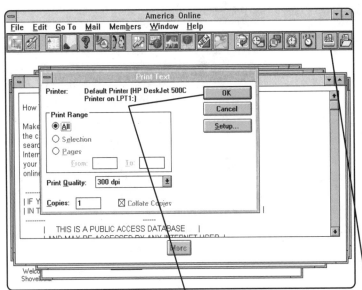

1. **Click** on the **Print icon** in the toolbar. The Print Text dialog box will appear.

2. **Click** on **OK**. The file will be printed.

## E-mailing Your Resume

If you are going to e-mail your resume now, you should have a copy handy. If not, you can just read through this section.

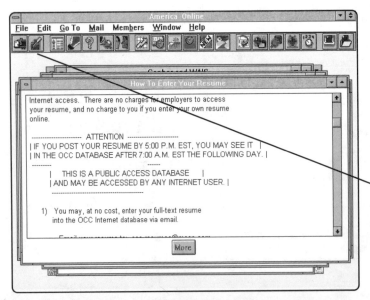

1. **Click** on the **Compose Mail icon** in the toolbar. The Compose Mail dialog box will appear.

2. **Type O.C.C.'s address**. It is in the file you just printed.

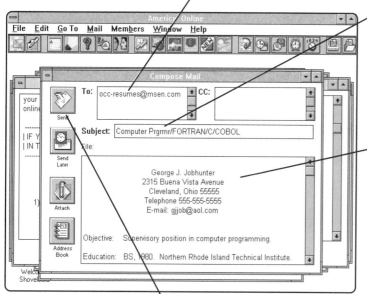

3. **Type** a **subject**. Be creative. The *subject will be the title of your resume* on the system. Make sure that it will catch your potential employer's eye!

4. **Type** (or **cut and paste** from a text file) your **resume** here. Be certain to include your address, phone number, and e-mail address. Since this a text file, you cannot format your resume as you can in a word-processing program. Keep the information clear and concise. Don't waste a potential employer's time.

5. **Click** on **Send**. Your resume is on its way!

## GOING BACK TO GOPHER & WAIS

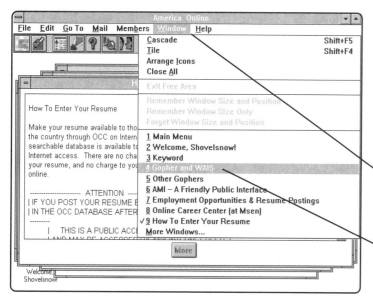

You can come back later to explore more of O.C.C.'s job listings. Now let's check out another great source of job-search information.

1. **Click** on **Window** in the menu bar. A pull-down menu will appear.

2. **Click** on **Gopher and WAIS**. The Gopher and WAIS dialog box will appear.

## FINDING ANOTHER GREAT SOURCE

AOL's editor's choice, Business and Employment, lists several excellent sources for job information. The RiceInfo Gopher, from Rice University in Texas, is one of the best.

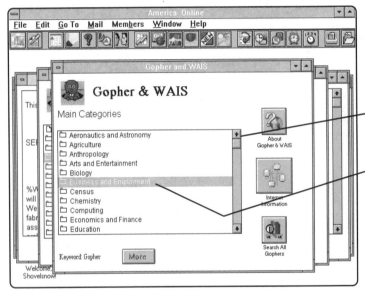

1. **Click repeatedly** on the ↑ to **scroll up** the list.

2. **Click twice** on **Business and Employment**. The Business and Employment dialog box will appear.

3. **Click twice** on **Jobs and Employment from RiceInfo**. The Jobs and Employment from RiceInfo dialog box will appear.

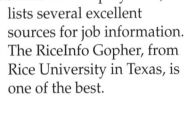

❖ RiceInfo lists dozens of job sources for you to explore. Let's look at one of the country's largest employers.

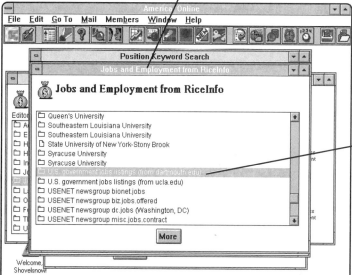

**4.** **Click repeatedly** on the ⬇ to **scroll down** the list.

**5.** **Click** on **More** to view more choices.

**6.** **Click twice** on **U.S. government jobs listings (from dartmouth.edu)**. The U.S. government jobs listings (from dartmouth.edu) dialog box will appear.

❖ Notice that this posting also contains a list of jobs in private industry with companies doing work for the government.

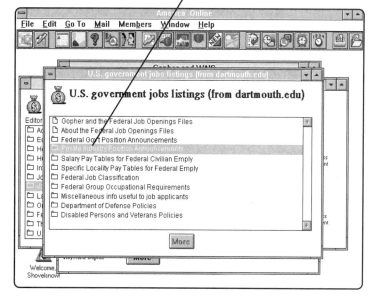

## TAKING STOCK

❖ Now that you've seen some of the many highways to job-hunting resources on Gopher, you may want to stop for a while, review any files you've saved, make some notes, and think about your next job-hunting move.

❖ Remember that like all other gopher resources, job lists change constantly. If you're actively looking for a job, you should recheck the most promising sources frequently. More importantly, act quickly when you find a job notice that looks good. Save the notice and go for it NOW! The listing could be removed within a few days.

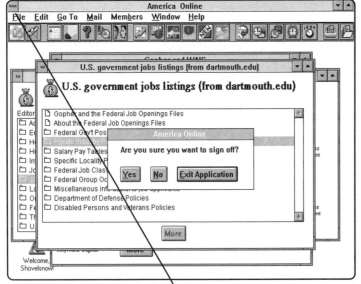

❖ No one can guarantee that you'll find the job of your dreams on the Internet. However, the range of opportunities probably beats the listings in your local newspaper hands-down.

## EXITING FROM AOL

1. **Click** on the ⊟ in the left corner of the AOL title bar. An America Online dialog box will appear.

2. **Click** on **Yes**. You will be disconnected from the online service, but the America Online program will still be running, **or Click** on **Exit Application** to both disconnect and exit from the America Online program.

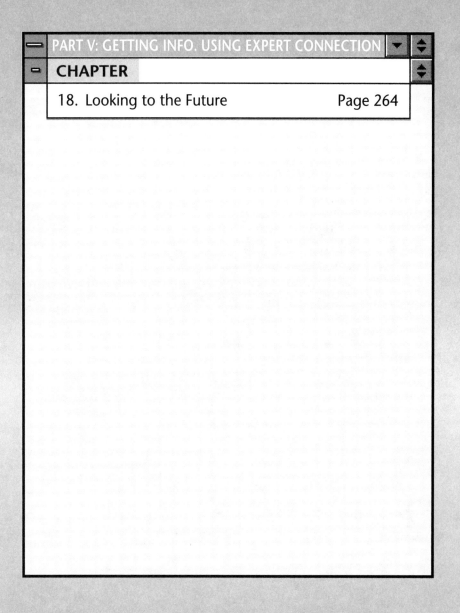

# Looking to the Future

America Online is light-years ahead of everyone else! At the time of this writing, there is absolutely no other service that makes it as easy and exciting to use the Internet. And the good news is that there is more to come. As this book went to press, AOL was feverishly working on providing even more Internet options. In addition to the e-mail, newsgroups, mailing lists, and Gopher and WAIS features that are already available, you will be able to use two other exciting Internet features, FTP and telnet, which together make up Expert Connection on AOL. FTP will allow you to send and receive document files and graphics, and telnet will provide you with direct connections to remote computers on the Internet. In this chapter, you will learn about the following:

❖ How FTP will allow you to send and receive files on the Internet
❖ How telnet will allow you to connect to a remote computer
❖ How to contact the authors if you have any questions about this book

## OPENING EXPERT CONNECTION

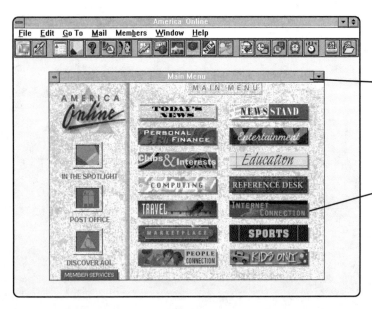

1. **Sign on to AOL** if you have not already done so.

2. **Click** on the **title bar** of the **Main Menu** just above the Welcome screen (not shown here). The Main Menu will appear.

3. **Click** on **Internet Connection**. The Internet Connection dialog box will appear.

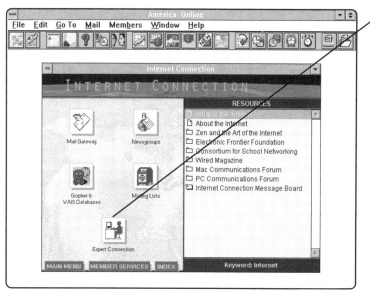

4. **Click** on **Expert Connection**. At the time this book went to press, the Expert Connection dialog box shown below appeared.

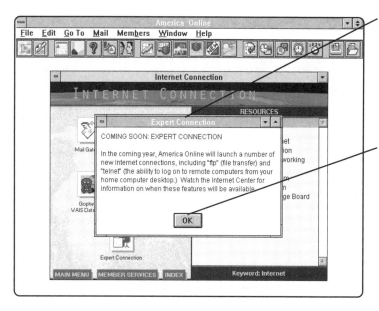

❖ The short note on Expert Connection shown here barely hints at the many interesting and useful things you'll be able to do with these services.

5. **Click** on **OK**. The dialog box will close. At some point in the near future, clicking on Expert Connection will open a whole new world of options!

## LEARNING ABOUT FTP

Thus far in AOL, you've been able to send e-mail to anyone on the Internet. However, you haven't been able to send a document created in Word, or WordPerfect, or Excel, for example. FTP, or *File Transfer Protocol*, will change that. (The recipient must have Word, or WordPerfect, or Excel, or a program that will convert the file in order to open the file on his computer.)

Host Computer Files

Your Computer

FTP also allows you to send and receive actual documents and graphics files between your computer and any other computer, regardless of whether the computers are the same type. For example, with FTP you can download a file from a UNIX machine or IBM's OS/2 operating system to your PC or Mac.

Exploring with AOL's FTP Will Be Easy, Fun — a Whole New World!

For technically oriented folks, the details of how the transfer is done are fascinating. For those of us more normal mortals, who cares how it's done? AOL's Expert Connection will do all the work for you. All you'll have to do is click here, click there, and voilá — you'll get the files you want. You'll be able to tap into a whole new world of software, text, and graphics files at sites around the globe.

## EXPLORING THE WORLD WITH TELNET

Telnet is very similar to FTP in the sense that you can connect directly to other computers on the Internet.

### Running Programs on a Remote Computer

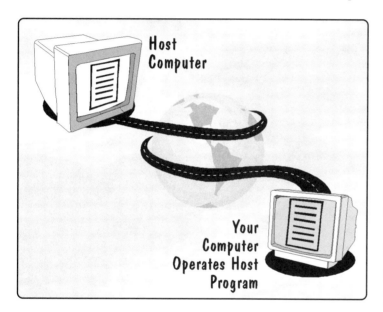

**Host Computer**

**Your Computer Operates Host Program**

What telnet does that FTP doesn't do is let you interact with programs that are running on a remote computer. The programs can be games, databases, job-information services, bulletin boards, or any other program that the remote computer's operator allows you to access.

### Cruising the Information Superhighway

We've all been hearing about the new "information superhighway," where you will be able to cruise around the world and have access to programs and computers almost anywhere. Today, telnet is what will make that possible.

### Let Us Hear from You

If you have comments or suggestions on how we can improve this book or our other books, we'd love to hear from you. Our AOL screen name is WRITE BKS.

# Index